cortez

la plata mtn

mountain ute
indian reservation

southern ute
indian reservation

FOUR CORNERS

os pos

shiprock

farmi

rock

hukai

ms tsaile

bn del

uerto wheatfield

blanca peak

helly

ort defiance

window
rock

crown point

santa fe

gallup

fort
wingate

mt. taylor

oh

ruins

cañoncito

zuñi

ramah

alamo

to fort sumner

st

Crow Man's people

By the same author

A butterfly sings to Pacaya

Bill Draper's scarecrow in the field at Twin Trails, Canyon del Muerto

NIGEL PRIDE

Crow Man's people

Three seasons with the Navajo

Constable · London

First published in Great Britain
by Constable and Company Limited
10 Orange Street London WC2H 7EG
Copyright © 1982 by Nigel Pride
ISBN 0 09 463600 1
Set in Linotron Baskerville 11 pt by
Rowland Phototypesetting Ltd
Bury St Edmunds, Suffolk
Printed in Great Britain by
St Edmundsbury Press
Bury St Edmunds

For my mother and father

My deepest gratitude to the
Draper family and others of
the Navajo people who showed
me such kindness. Of them and
their lands in the high country
of North East Arizona my
memories will last for ever.

Contents

Illustrations

12 · Illustrations

Part I
Summer

Far below, pale silver sand edged the shallow wash which cut its way along the canyon floor. Two shadows the size of ants moved for a moment on the water and then were lost in the distortions of the afternoon heat. They were Navajo horses.

Moving further away from the canyon wall the two horses walked out into the brilliant sunlight, one white, the other black. I looked down into the depths of Canyon del Muerto, each view seeming more dramatic and magical than the last. Smoothed and just faintly damped with water the wash, lined with its cottonwood and willow, meandered in a contrast of simplicity against the canyon's monumental walls.

On the canyon's west vertical cliffs the swallows and martins had pockmarked the strata bands with nesting holes, the birds flashing across the space below me. Scoured and sliced by floods over eons of time the canyon walls fell hundreds of feet to the wash. Opposite, the east rim was raked with giant fissures and red buttresses of shining rock sharply drawn against the brilliant blue sky.

For nearly two years I had written persistently to the Bureau of Indian Affairs, first in Washington and then at Window Rock in Arizona, trying to make arrangements for me to live with a Navajo family. I had always been deeply interested in the Indian cultures of the Americas, past and present, and on my return from Guatemala and Mexico where I had studied the Pre-Hispanic cultures, and in particular that of the Maya, I had decided to learn something of a tribe of Indians living in the south-west of the United States, the Navajo.

On an earlier drive from California to New York I had crossed through the northern section of the Navajo reservation, a land of unbelievable primitive grandeur. I had seen few of the inhabitants then but those I had seen and the dramatic scale of their lands had stimulated my imagination and interest. Wind- and rain-sculpted mesas and monolithic buttes rising up from deserts of red earth are perhaps the most easily recognizable features of that region, but the Navajo lands also had spectacular mountains and forests, and great canyons carved by seasonal rivers.

East of the Grand Canyon I had come down into sun-baked lands whose desolate wastes were punctuated with the unique forms of the log-walled Navajo home, the six-sided hogan. The reservation lands stretched from Arizona east into New Mexico and north into southern Utah, covering 25,000 square miles. And the Navajo, unlike any other Indian tribe in the United States, had actually thrived and multiplied. They are the largest of all the tribes in North America.

These facts, the Navajos' obvious vitality and determination to survive and retain their identity in spite of the dominating society around them, intrigued me even more. Navajos call themselves 'Dine', The People, and are still as closely related to their land and the old religious respect of nature as they had been in the times before the coming of the white man. The Navajo nation now numbers around 136,000. They remain a pastoral society, and the problems of such an arid land supporting an ever-increasing population are considerable. At present the Navajo are among the poorest Indians in the United States although the discoveries on their land of large deposits of coal, natural gas, oil, and particularly uranium may eventually offer the Navajos a means of sustaining their cultural and economic independence.

Change was and is inevitable. In many ways The People have proved their ability to adapt, but they are, as are most other tribes of North America, encapsulated by the world's most advanced industrial nation. Being so affected by and adhering to spiritual values completely unlike those of white America, pressures from the surrounding non-Indian peoples could finally break the strength of the last great tribe north of the Rio Grande. Or, with their intelligent evaluations of the problems of non-Indians and careful adjustments of theirs, they could significantly influence the social development of our own.

I expected to find evidence of the problems of transition and perhaps of the confusion of young Navajos exposed to white attitudes. For pressures are at their severest now and the generation who in youth rode horseback and who accepted the ancient ways of The People without question is dying out.

Young Navajos are bewildered with choice but show distinct signs of checking against a headlong rush into cultural oblivion. Besides the obvious infringement of their old values I was uncertain what I would discover about the Navajo but for some almost unaccountable reason I felt compelled to find out and, as far as possible, in a simple and unobtrusive way.

I waited and waited. A never-ending stream of letters crossed the Atlantic, falling into the bureaucratic machine of the Department of the Interior. Replies were irregular but always polite and on the surface helpful but after eighteen months I seemed no nearer my goal than I had been when I started my requests.

It seemed to me the best way to understand the Navajo would be through a direct relationship with a family. In that association I might see some of their contemporary problems through their eyes. As I continued my correspondence with the Bureau of Indian Affairs I realized more and more the difficulties of establishing such contacts. Who would bother to make such negotiations on my behalf between a Navajo household and me, an unknown quantity six thousand miles away?

Navajos are a reserved and conservative people. Outsiders with some knowledge and experience of Navajo manners were pessimistic about my venture. Anthropologists and historians, casual visitors to the reservation and students of American Indian culture offered little hope of my success.

'They'll never talk to you. Navajos won't have anything to do with white people. They call them Anglos and aren't too friendly to say the least.'

This sort of statement did little to encourage me but knowing that Navajos, historically with some justification, had little liking for white Americans and viewed their motives with suspicion, I felt that if I could achieve the first step of introduction I would be all right. Not being American might at least have curiosity value even though I was obviously white.

I worked hard at my own optimism constantly, more determined than ever and at last in May 1979 I received a letter from the administrative capital of the Navajo nation, Window Rock, Arizona. A Navajo employee of the Bureau of Indian Affairs working in the Department of Education had suggested that members of his own family, in the Canyon de Chelly area, would be willing to be hosts upon my arrival there in July 1979. Other professional commitments in my life dictated the periods of time available to me for first-hand research among the Navajo. With this far-from-detailed offer I began immediately to make the practical arrangements for the intended summer stay in Arizona. A good friend in California lent me a Volkswagen truck and he and others supplied camping equipment. All I had to do was fly to San Francisco with my nine-year-old son, Nathan, bus a further three hundred miles into the Sierras of northern California, collect the vehicle and drive to Arizona. Nothing was simple but in effect that was what happened and early in July I reached the reservation.

My son said nothing but took in everything as I swung the truck around the potholes of the road that held the ragged Navajo township of Chinle in some semblance of order. After driving eleven hundred miles from northern California in two-and-a-half days we were there, on the Navajo reservation, full of a mixture of apprehension and excitement.

It was midday Saturday, and everyone was either buying goods or just enjoying the opportunity of gossip and personal display. Chinle had grown into a commercial and administrative centre as a result of the Bureau of Indian Affairs having established social welfare, medical and education offices there. Originally it was known only for its two trading posts, but now its civic role and the housing and consumer needs of B.I.A. employees has followed the pattern of Window Rock to become an important centre of the northeast section of the reservation. Tourism has contributed greatly to this expansion with the Canyon de Chelly area designated as a National Monument in 1931, although the 130-square-mile area still belongs to the Navajos. Unlike the much earlier settlers of this region, the Anazazi or their present-day descendants, the Pueblo Indians of New Mexico, the People have never built formal villages. Navajos live in small scattered family units which form a loose identity as the family increases in a particular area, but this never develops further because of their pastoral way of life and strong personal need for independence. Their social pattern of life has caused and continues to cause significant problems for economical and political development.

The need for consumer goods and general hardware draws out the families from their remote hogans along the mesas and canyon rims. Some Navajos would have driven perhaps a hundred miles or more with their children and grandparents packed into high fat-tyred pick-up trucks. Indians literally spilled from the trucks, and others walked along the road.

Suddenly after the immense spaces and sparse population of the journey such an explosion of humanity was unnerving. I felt very much the white man surrounded by Indians, and I was. Many of the trucks carried rifles, the weapons hanging on racks behind the crowded passengers, and behind these, covering the rear view cab windows, were plastic sunshields emblazoned with bucking horses and mountain scenery.

Women and children dominated the traffic. Old women sat resolute in the open back of the trucks wearing velveteen blouses and flounced skirts and a great amount of silver and turquoise jewellery, while granddaughters with long black hair and cowboy hats drove eight-cylinder engines with wild enthusiasm. There was an air of comfortable and natural authority about the Navajo womenfolk and I saw at once the outward signs of the ease of their authority in this matrilineal society. Through the female line comes the inheritance of family fortune, and children are born for their mother's clan.

Dust was flying everywhere from trucks' manoeuvres on the dirt side-roads and parking lots in front of the gas stations and stores. Pick-up trucks have become something of a cult throughout the west but nowhere are they quite so flamboyant as on the Navajo reservation. Modern 'horses' ridden with panache and enthusiasm they might seem but their role is realistic and practical. Without them the Indians would find contemporary life unworkable. Journeys across the Navajo lands are long and difficult and away from interstate highways the roads are unpaved and virtually impassable in winter even with four-wheel drive. Trucks make many things possible, especially schooling and medical services.

Looking around at the big hats, dark copper faces, guns, the unexpected numbers of Indians and their dignity, my thoughts were running wild. How on earth would I manage to become part of all this? Had I made a very expensive mistake in coming all this distance without the secure knowledge that I would in principle be accepted? I had not dared wait for further detailed confirmation in England, for another delay would have meant waiting another year before beginning the project. Now, standing in the sun outside Garcia's Trading Post, I realized the tenuousness of my position.

Oil from my truck's damaged rear axle bearing was leaking into the thick dust and I felt sick in the stomach. God, I thought in a state of nervous exhaustion, we're going to need a good line in miracles to survive this venture.

'Well, there seem to be a lot of Indians, Dad. Can I have a drink now?' Nathan could probably make this whole thing work I thought. In calculating the initial reserve and possibly the suspicion of the Navajo towards Anglo visitors I had felt that my son would not only have a unique opportunity to experience at first hand another people's way of life but because of the Navajos' natural unreserved love of children he would make their acceptance of us a lot easier. The easy way he had made friends among the Indian children in Mexico and Guatemala showed that his role among the Navajo at the beginning of our stay would be an important one.

'Yes,' I said, looking down at the spreading stain of oil. 'We'll get something to drink in a minute.'

Outside the offices of the Bureau of Indian Affairs I realized my arrival had been further ill-timed – it was closed until Monday. We made camp in the cottonwood grove at the edge of town. Resting in the shade of the national park's campground, waiting for the weekend to pass, I watched the tourist campers arriving and departing. Camper trucks and trailers larger than two hogans put together were parked among the trees complete with awnings, televisions and interiors carpeted and decorated like rooms of southern California tract homes.

It was hot. Dry bleaching heat of the high deserts shimmered back from dry parched rock. In the open places sunlight mercilessly exposed every grain of earth and last year's silvered débris of the fall. Among the cottonwood trees Navajo families cruised by in the never-ending variations of pick-up truck styling. They observed the Anglos at play. There was live entertainment – better than T.V., almost as good as the discourse and horseplay down around the trading post.

Winchester rifles gleamed dully in the cab racks and the dark faces beneath big feather-decorated hats filled the trucks' open windows. Adults displayed few signs of enjoyment or distaste but children's behaviour was an interesting mixture of uninhibited curiosity and peculiar self-containment. Navajo grandmothers, sometimes perched on a box or spare tyre in the back of the trucks, seemed indifferent to the inelegant sights of white women of their own age sporting luminous pink bermuda shorts and hair rollers.

Perhaps the aspect of social behaviour that surprised me most at this introduction to the Navajo was that of the young unmarried women and teenage girls of this matrilineal society. The young women's manner appeared delicately balanced between assertive, enthusiastic emancipation and unquestioned inherent superiority.

Nathan came round the side of the packed Volkswagen in a headlong rush. He was out of breath and excited. 'They want me to go with them in the truck. They're going swimming in the wash up the canyon. Can I go Dad?'

I slowed him down a little and asked who 'they' were.

'Those Indians over there. Look, out there by the fence.'

A truck bursting with Navajo children and a few adults was parked in the trees about a hundred yards away. I had noticed the group earlier enjoying what seemed to be a lively weekend picnic.

'Can I go, please? They're very nice. I've been playing with them.' Nathan danced about in wild anticipation.

Well, I thought, he's done it again. We've only been here a few hours and he's about to disappear off into the canyon with a truckful of Navajos. Would I ever manage such an easy and immediate access to Indian life? I doubted it. At least *his* adventure had begun. He could find out things for himself now.

'They said they'll bring me back at five o'clock, Dad.'

'Yes, all right. Take a towel. You can swim in the shorts you're wearing. And be careful. Don't fall out of the truck.'

He was gone before I had finished, a blur of skinny brown legs racing towards the Navajo. They pulled him into the back and the truck ripped away in a cloud of dust and children's squeals.

Oil continued to seep from the fractured axle bearing on to the inside face of the wheel and tyre and then down into the red-baked earth. It was going to cost money and out here in the middle of the reservation repair facilities were far from plentiful. My budget was extremely frugal, the limits finely set. Damn and blast, what an irritation to have to bother with right at the start of all this.

Before beginning my journey, I had bought a sheet of thick plywood from a lumberyard and covered in the back of the Volkswagen truck. The board lay across the open back and I had screwed it to the top edge of the truck sides to form a storage area about 5′ × 6′6″. A lengthways section along the nearside edge about 20″ wide I hinged and secured with padlocks. This enabled me to lower the truck's side panel and raise the hinged flap to form an area to cook on and gain easier access to goods stored inside the otherwise-sealed compartment. When closed the hinged lid and the remaining area of plywood became a sleeping platform where Nathan and I could, if necessary, roll out our sleeping bags and sleep quite comfortably under the stars.

Later that afternoon while lying on this platform trying to ignore the pungent smell of axle oil and the persistent quests of three over-active flies, I caught sight of the Navajo swimming party returning my son.

The truck stopped only long enough for him to jump down and then disappeared from my view. Nathan's head popped up over the tailgate and he climbed up beside me.

'I had a great time. They gave me some water melon too. We went right into this canyon – it was amazing. We went right through the water lots of times. One truck was stuck and it was sinking into the quicksand. Only the top was sticking out. The engine was right under, you couldn't see it.'

Nathan's shoulders were burnt dark red, his ears were full of sand and there were rings of sore flesh around the tops of his thighs where the wet shorts had rubbed.

'Boy, the canyon was terrific, Dad. You should see those cliffs, they go straight up in the air. We went for miles along the wash. One boy fell off the back of the truck into the water but he was all right. Everybody laughed at him.'

On Monday morning I located the Education Department of the B.I.A. in Chinle and met a softly spoken lady from Memphis, Tennessee. Jean Combs, a white employee of the B.I.A. for most of her working life, had only a few months to go before retiring from her final post as Education Program Administrator of the Chinle Agency.

My earlier enquiries to the Navajo Area Office at Window Rock had been forwarded to her and she in turn had recommended certain Navajos working in the B.I.A. as possible sources of help and interest. One of these, she said, a William Draper, had agreed to make arrangements within his own family, but the final letter explaining details of this offer had arrived in England after my departure for Arizona and so until that moment I had not enjoyed such assurance.

This explanation had a marvellously calming effect. William Draper, however, had gone to a conference at Flagstaff and would not return until the end of the week.

While I took the Volkswagen truck to one of the two mechanics in Chinle, Jean Combs was to phone William Draper in Flagstaff and he in turn would call his brother Francis at the Fire Department in Chinle and arrange for him to take us to their parents at Del Muerto, nine miles north of Chinle.

At the garage set back on the dusty strip running the length of the main road the oil leak was diagnosed as the sign of a broken oil seal on a 'busted wheel bearing' and if I left the vehicle there it could be fixed by late afternoon.

More than pleased at the comparative ease of progress so far Nathan and I walked the hot and arduous couple of miles back to the cottonwoods – and waited.

Around midday, Nathan's rambling through the trees had attracted the attention of a Navajo. After being informed quite precisely by Nathan that 'my Daddy is in Arizona to write something about the Navajo,' he came over and introduced himself.

'I'm Eddie Tso. I hear you're interested in my people. That son of yours, he's some boy.'

The Navajo was, I guessed, in his middle thirties, simply dressed in jeans, T-shirt, cowboy boots and a western straw hat.

'Yeh, originally I come from Pinon. It's about twenty or thirty miles west of here. You know it?'

I had seen the name on the map, a black dot actually well within the area designated as the Hopi Reservation.

'I live in California now. Me, I'm training in computer techniques. I'm doing pretty good over there.'

We sat underneath a tree that rustled dryly in the hot wind. Eddie's views were interesting in several ways, not least that he was a Navajo who had found it necessary to leave the reservation and integrate himself in Anglo society.

'You see, firstly, I became a Christian, the Presbyterian church. We found God six years ago and me and my family are much happier now. I come out here about once a year to visit my people and look around at my old home. Me, I still need to see the canyons and mesas. I miss this stuff in California.'

Would he ever return to Arizona and the reservation, I asked him.

'Well I'd like to, really, but I think my religion would be held against me by my people over there. Employment would be a bigger problem. I don't know. You see, my schooling wasn't too good and I reckon I would need to have graduate qualifications out here to really get a good job.

'Most white and blue collar type jobs are with the government and tribal administration. I think I stand more chance in California.'

Eddie Tso called out to his small son who was about to jump from a tree into a camp garbage can and then turned back to me looking somewhat sad at his own reflective talk.

'Anyway, my wife wouldn't like to chop wood no more in the winter. Hey, we're used to running water, electricity, refrigerators and all that stuff.

'Drinking is a big problem you know with some Navajos. I think it wears down a lot of the young people's energy and they get depressed with the unemployment problems on the reservation. Me – I think the church would help break down this liquor business. Bootleggers sure don't help any.

'You know what the law is, the sale, possession, and drinking of alcohol on the reservation is strictly forbidden but down here it's just like the old prohibition days. This bootlegger down here in Chinle – he's a rich man now, makes big profits all the time.

Yes, now and again they catch him selling stuff and put him in jail but someone else takes over until he gets out. There's always a lot of people want liquor.'

At four o'clock a national parks ranger offered me a ride into town to collect the truck. At the garage, when I asked if the vehicle was ready, the black owner cheerfully answered my question with his own.

'Hey man, do you have the part? We don't have the part. Hey, this is foreign, man!'

Trying to assume a relaxed manner in accord with the general theme around me, I said that I would try to get the replacement bearing from the local auto factors myself so that he could replace it.

At the parts dealer I was told it wasn't in stock but could be 'bussed' from Gallup in two or three days. I had no alternative, and arranged the order and then, assuming that the wheel would hold out until then, drove carefully to my appointment with Jean Combs and Francis Draper.

From the B.I.A. offices I followed Jean to Francis Draper's home, a small framed house about a quarter-mile north in the area set aside for bureau employees. At the heavy clang of the metal garden gate Francis Draper came out to the porch step and we were introduced. His English was poor but he was enthusiastically loud in his speech.

'So, you come all this way, eh. I think I know about some of those things you want to know maybe. My brother Bill he mentioned something sometime back. Nobody called me today. That Fire Department, they don't relay messages to us – unless it's an emergency.'

Francis was dressed neatly in the usual western style and looked in his late forties and one of the most noticeable effects was the enormous silver belt buckle engraved 'Area Champion Bronc Rider'.

'Bill most likely told my Mom out at the ranch that you would visit them pretty soon. I guess that's about it.'

I thanked Jean and she left me with Francis to sort out the further details of my stay. Still feeling rather like babes in arms, Nathan and I followed our new host into the house and luxuriated in the willingness of Francis to talk about his people and help us start my project. His young wife Ella came in shortly afterwards with their three-and-a-half-month-old son and following these new introductions we all left for Francis' parents' home.

We followed the newly paved road which runs north to Tsaile from the bridge across the Chinle Wash at the mouth of Canyon de Chelly. After ten miles we were just east of the rim of Canyon del Muerto which sloped up to a gently rolling grass ridge cleared of the normal covering of juniper and piñon. Way back from the highway nestling in the lee of the ridge was the Draper ranch.

We rattled up the pink earth track, past a cluster of corrals and sun-bleached wooden shelters for horses and cattle, through a large gate and into the fenced yard which surrounded the small low-roofed home of Garnet and Henry Draper.

By this time I was as nervous as a lizard on a flat rock and was desperately worried about our reception. Perhaps the old couple would prefer not to bother with Anglo strangers! How on earth would I communicate?

Behind the frame buildings, fifty yards up the slope, was a log-walled hogan with an earth dome roof. Its logs were old twisted juniper trunks locked at the hogan's six corners with carefully cut notches. It was an older style Navajo home, not replaced by buildings of board and roofing felt.

In the shade of the low east-facing porch, the old couple sat with their dogs. We got down from the truck and Francis spoke to his parents in Navajo and then introduced Nathan and myself. I asked Francis to explain to his mother and father why we had come seven thousand miles to visit the Navajo.

To my great relief the old lady smiled and spoke in English. 'Bill Draper, my son, he said you might come one day. You are welcome. You can stay as long as you want. We don't care. Everything is all right with us.'

Henry, her husband, a thin old man with baggy trousers and thick pebble glasses, spoke in Navajo to Francis. He was far less fluent with his English but he screwed up his face and waving his gnarled hand towards the pastures just beyond the hogan he said, 'Yes, sure, everything is O.K. You set up camp anywhere you like.'

We had arrived. Much of the anxiety and uncertainty diminished in those moments and I thanked our hosts. They

Henry (84) and Garnet Draper (79) at their son Bill's home at Ganado

laughed and like Francis and Jean Combs before them, recognized our relief at finding a real home among the Navajo.

I drove Francis back to Chinle and then returned to the ranch to set up our camp. On the open treeless bluff we put up the yellow tent. It sat square and pugnacious against the setting sun and a distant long flat-topped mesa with its vermilion edge.

Nathan ran off to play with the dogs and then followed the goats the old man was herding in from the far southern end of the pasture. I looked around, secure at last, and felt that we had opened the first line of communication. We now had friends among the Navajo. Early days, with many problems to solve, but there seemed now a real chance to succeed.

About a mile away was the rim of Canyon del Muerto, 'Canyon of the Dead', the west branch of the Canyon de Chelly complex. On the canyon bottom Garnet and Henry Draper had a number of small fields where they grew corn, squash, alfalfa and a small orchard of peaches and plums. This I knew from the Francis' descriptions and it was possible that we would be able to see these places quite soon.

Navajos owning land in the canyons often lived there and worked the small fields during the summers. Irrigation with water from the wash after the spring thaw made it possible to make four cuts of hay and grow good strong corn.

Henry Draper said that he would take me down on his next visit and I could see how The People lived in the canyon. Cliff dwellings of the earlier inhabitants, the Anazazi, still remained on the ledges beneath the giant overhangs of the canyon walls. It was all there waiting to be explored.

Anglos are forbidden to enter the canyons unless they are accompanied by official Navajo guides. Visitors are, for the most part, taken into the canyon only by four-wheel drive vehicles during the summer months when the wash is usually very low and access is possible. Even during those months the shallow wash covers the broad canyon floor in a thin deceptive film and areas of quicksand take a yearly toll of unwary drivers. People who seem most often to come to grief are Navajos not from the immediate area who take advantage of the privilege of being free to enter the canyon but are unfamiliar with the proper trail. Large smooth areas of sandy wash bed look inviting tracks for testing a truck's mobility but those often turn out to be vehicle graves.

From the Chinle wash bridge I had seen a large yellow truck buried in the wet sand up to the seats of the cab. Others just sink slowly out of sight while the owners watch.

Our hosts, the old Navajo couple, had lived through times of dramatic changes. They had been born at the end of the Indian warrior society and had grown up within the Navajo circle, observing the white culture beyond the borders of their lands and when convenient using it. Childhood was shepherding and horse-riding with occasional trips to the lonely trading post on the back of the family wagon. Two World Wars in which whites had fought each other had come and gone. Navajos had fought alongside white Americans in the Pacific theatre of war and when Navajo soldiers returned to the reservation they brought new ideas, new tastes for consumer goods and often strange white social attitudes. Paved roads had started to make travel easier across the lands of The People and with these had come tractors, pick-up trucks and packaged washing detergent.

Garnet and Henry still relied upon many of the old ways and were now too old to change. They were without running water and electricity but relied upon many of the contemporary gadgets and machinery to make their old age a little easier.

Henry was eighty-four as far as Garnet could tell – and she had seen seventy-nine years. Neither looked that old, especially Garnet, whose bearing was that of an acknowledged matriarchal family head and a well-respected figure among the people in the area. Old Henry drove his big blue pick-up and looked after about forty beef cattle and a small number of sheep and goats.

In the past, the Drapers, like most Navajo, had kept a large herd of sheep but now with their children grown up and living away from the canyon, herding sheep had become too much work. The few they owned now were kept for their own eating needs. I had seen three or four fresh sheep skins drying on the corral fence and from the crossbeams of the open-sided shelter near the house, strips of bloody meat hung turning dark and dry.

Almost unnoticed, night had come and in the darkness were the smells of sage and dry grass. In the distance a light flickered briefly on and then like the very last thin blur of red along the horizon it was gone and we were left in a soft purple black. Nathan's shadow on the tent wall was a peculiar living thing set within the block of orange yellow light that was our present home. The tent sat on the bluff in ridiculous and luminous disharmony, its pressure-lamp hissing insensitively against the gentler night breeze.

I looked up at the sky for a long time. Its clear enormity was waking with stars. Out in the distance, across the mesa, were all the spectres of my uncertainties cast in fragile form.

Old Garnet Draper had lit the oil lamp, lighting the porch for a moment as Henry took a last look at the land and then it was gone. I walked back to the yellow tent on the bluff.

The following morning, impatient to check our new surroundings, we drove along the west rim of the canyon, stopping at the overlooks to familiarize ourselves with the world below the mesas.

We stood at an elevation of about 6,000 feet with all the clarity of landscape definition that such an altitude affords. Chinle, down in the valley, sits at 5,500 feet above sea level and the canyon's rims rise to around 7,000 feet along its eastern extremities. It was 50 million years ago when waters flowing from the Chuska Mountains, thirty miles to the east, started the pattern of erosion which has carved the 20-mile-long canyon complex through the Defiance Plateau to a depth in some places of 1,500 feet.

Juniper and piñon pine grew to the very rim of the canyon and withdrew from its edge only when the uppermost layer of conglomerate rock proved in some areas too ungracious a host. The red sandstone walls of Canyon del Muerto contained a world which was the symbolic heart of Navajo history.

Shadows and cracks pulsed with colour and heat. Wide plunging stains of manganese and iron oxide, brought to the surface by water spilling over the rims, were the reminders of winter's freezing rain and snow. Now deceptively passive, the wash below would then resume in earnest the eternal cutting and shaping of the rock monuments which had provided homes and fortresses for both the Navajo and their predecessors.

Our camp lay drenched in windless heat until mid-afternoon when a fresh breeze whipped up the dust and drove the goats further across the mesa top. We were without shade on the bluff except for whatever the tent itself allowed and we struggled in the wind to make additional shade with a tarpaulin and ropes strung on the south side of our poor shelter.

Water had to be collected from Chinle, a round trip of twenty miles, where we filled our five-gallon plastic container and said goodbye to showers and normal washing. Garnet and Henry Draper like most other Navajos had a metal tank in which their domestic water was kept and when this had been used they

Navajo rider starting the trail to the rim of Canyon de Muerto (see p. 140)

would hoist it on to the truck and drive to Chinle for a refill. Most Navajos would have to haul water far greater distances than that during the dry months. Such things as running water, showers and flush toilets were enjoyed by very few – and those, most probably, were employees of the B.I.A. at the widely spaced government agency centres.

By Navajo standards the Drapers were successful. They had nearly a thousand acres and, under a tribal government scheme, had been able to clear an extensive area along the bluff of its native covering of juniper and piñon. Once cleared the land had been fenced and seeded with a type of grass that could survive low rainfall. It had been three years before cattle had been able to graze the newly established pasture but now a herd of about forty steers were able to bring in a steady and profitable income. A windmill pump set high up at the north end of the land brought water from a deep underground well to the surface for the cattle but as yet this was unsuitable for human consumption.

Beef ranching on any significant scale is totally undeveloped within the reservation and will remain so until the Navajo tribal government is able to invest more in artesian wells and irrigation schemes.

Sheep, goats and cattle had their water supply but we, like the Drapers, sipped our supply frugally and washed everything in the same water.

Francis came to see us that evening and after showing Nathan and me the shelves of silver cups, trophies and belt buckles he had won at rodeo events he settled down and talked of his early days.

'All we did was herd sheep. Riding horses all the time up here on the mesa and down in the canyons. When I was a boy we rode bareback most times. I never had no saddle then.

'Sometimes we go down to the trading post in Chinle with my folks. I used to look at all that stuff on the shelves there. I really used to think about those things a lot but I didn't have no money.

'One day I said to the man – he spoke good Navajo, I really want a pair of cowboy boots, a big hat and some jeans and one of those western shirts.

'"Well," said this trading post man, "if you want things like that you'll have to get a job that pays money."

'"All right," I say, "how do I get a job?"

'"Well, if you really do want a job, I'll see what I can do. I know a man in Ganado who might help you."'

From this began a series of events which led Francis to travel from Chinle to Wyoming, then to Seattle, Washington, and on up to Anchorage, Alaska.

'You know,' Francis spat at the big antlered deer skull lying near the truck, 'I didn't speak no English then, not a small bit, nothing. They fix me up with this job on the railroad up there in Alaska. One minute I was riding a horse on the reservation and then I was in this plane. I was scared. They pinned a label on my shirt with my name on and where I was going. Hell, I didn't know anything. That was the first time I ever been in a plane.

'We was replacing this narrow railroad track up there with a wider one. I worked with whites and Negroes and Eskimoes. We got on pretty good. I worked hard and they liked me.

'This boss I had – he looked after me a lot and told me to save my money and only spend a little bit on clothes.

'They told me I had to work up there for three months but after two and a half I told them I had to come back to the reservation. So I was released from that job and they told me to just wear old clothes so that nobody would notice me and put all my stuff in a trunk. I was labelled up again and the boss said I should sort of keep out of people's way so I wouldn't get robbed or led astray.

'Even when I got to Seattle and met some other Navajos who were pretty noisy and drunk I just kept by myself.

'It was funny when I got to Gallup because I met my brother walking down the street. We got really excited at seeing each other again and we decided to take my monies and buy a truck.

'In those days there was only a few cars and trucks out here. Hardly any. The roads were just dirt or graded – not like now. Pretty soon we go down to the Ford dealers right there in Gallup and bought this brand new Ford pick-up. I couldn't drive then but my brother he could and we got to Chinle really late that night.

'Well we was shouting and yelling and we drove up to the hogan of another brother and honked that old horn in the darkness. We carried on makin' all this noise until someone just opened the hogan door, just a little bit. They were scared. So we yelled some more and laughed until they knew who it was – then we all had a good time meeting like that.

'In a little while me and my brother went up to my Mom and Dad's hogan and did the same thing. My Mom was really scared, they think we was ghosts or something and they wouldn't come out at all. So in the end I had to shout out my name so they knew it was me and then they came out. They was so happy to see me – even though it was midnight. They couldn't believe that Ford was mine – they just kept walking round it.

'That's how I came back to the reservation from Alaska and after that time I used to do a lot with vehicles and did pretty good in the rodeos too.'

At mid-morning we reached the entrance to the canyon where Henry Draper got out of the truck and turned the front hubs into four-wheel drive. Henry wanted to collect a load of hay from the cabin on his land up by Twin Trails and he had invited us to come along.

Nathan and I stood in the back of the truck holding on to the rails of the high extended sides while Garnet sat up front with Henry. Water in the wash at this point was almost non-existent and the flat bed of sand looked like a broad golden highway snaking back into the canyon. Riding across the first flats was comfortable but as we entered the canyon proper, water glistened in deeper troughs and ragged channels and we lurched over sharp edges of baked sand and stone-filled hollows.

Views of the canyon from its bottom were even more spectacular than from the rim and riding the truck like a chariot I felt unashamedly wildly excited. Sometimes the trail was clearly visible by the tracks of earlier vehicles crossing the flat moist sand but in some places the wash had spread a thin cool film and covered the clues. On these stretches old Henry put his foot down and the water flew up in sunlit sprays.

Giant pink ramparts of the canyon walls began to loom over us, the cracks and hollows creating a never-ending pattern of dark and light, line and mass.

Standing there in the back of the racing truck, I could hardly be blamed for feeling just a little superior and far more fortunate than other whites whose limited access to the canyon was a formal guided party arrangement.

Heat vibrated from the sand and stone. The temperature was in the upper nineties, and the sun slapped down on the steel of the cab roof and burned our hands. Nathan's hair was already bleaching and my head ached with the glare. Suddenly we swerved out to the centre of the wash, cutting through the channels of water and then drove up and over abrupt shelves of rock and sand into narrow tunnels of shade among cottonwood trees. Green and quivering, the leaves flicked the truck and we hung on – laughing as we ducked beneath the overhanging branches.

Even higher, the canyon walls rose above us, great soaring slabs, uncannily vertical and smooth as though split clean with a giant's axe. Behind tall bull-grass and grey willow we occasionally glimpsed an earth-roofed hogan, its colour identical to the rock above it. Small box canyons protected tiny patches of corn or miniature fields where a horse stood heat-drowsy. A world so quiet, its silence rarely interrupted by more than the squeaks of martins and swallows – or that more subtle sound, the delicate whirring of busy hummingbirds.

At the junction of Canyon de Chelly and Canyon del Muerto we took the western branch and entered the Canyon of the Dead. More cottonwoods softened the canyon floor and the wash widened and narrowed as we moved upstream. On the northwest wall of the canyon we passed several small Anazazi ruins, their earth colours making a natural harmony of both natural and man-made structures.

Antelope House appeared next, a large multi-roomed structure in the cliff with its easily recognized rock-paintings of animals. Then as we passed through a narrow defile the trail became steadily more demanding both for vehicle and driver. Outcrops of rock edged the trail causing us to pitch over at an angle that frightened me but had little effect upon Nathan. He jumped from one side of the truck to the other determined not to miss anything.

We crossed and re-crossed the wash, moving from the centre to the edges of the canyon and back again. An elderly Navajo slithered under a fence as he hurried to catch up with his flock of sheep and goats. Jumping gracefully from a high bank the animals started across the canyon floor. Henry honked and shouted at the bobbing heads and tails and then we lurched on down the trail.

Looking back down the canyon from the direction we had come I watched the old Navajo follow the flock across the broad wash. In the distance the sheep looked like a tiny string of pearls compared to the enormous backdrop of pink and red stone cliffs. My reverie was short-lived, ended by an abrupt drop through a narrow section of the canyon which was packed with boulders and flood débris. Like a tank we charged up an eroded bank and rolled on through a grove of silver-green willow and passed a small hogan sheltering in the shade of a large twisted cottonwood. Scattering in a white fluffy shower, some of the trees' seeds fell into the wash and floated away towards Antelope House.

It had taken one hour and twenty minutes to reach the Draper's cabin at Twin Trails.

In the shade of the cottonwood were two small structures, one a shed containing a small tractor and general farm implements and supplies. The other was a neat log-walled cabin with a wood stove, a double bed and a collection of pots and pans, a small table and a couple of chairs. Facing east the cabin looked out towards the wash and behind it a canyon wall rose six hundred feet.

Henry Draper's first act was to bring out an old mattress from the cabin and throw it on an ancient single iron bedstead standing on a little rise underneath the cottonwood. Garnet sat on a folding chair in the shade while Henry went over to look at his small orchard of peach and plum trees. We followed the old man and he pointed out that an animal had been eating the peaches and he had set a gin trap. Although sprung the trap was empty, there was no sign of the culprit or any indication of its kind. Raccoons and skunks were common enough in the canyon but Henry said it was just as likely to be a dog.

Joining Garnet we caught a little of the cooler breeze from the wash and sat for a while. Henry lay on the old bed looking up through the cottonwood branches.

I was curious about the wildlife of the area and asked Garnet if there were snakes in the canyon.

'Ha, we don't see rattlesnakes down here but now and again bullsnakes come round the cabin. They go out through that grass round the fields.

'Just the other day this big bullsnake, it was really a long one, went up the side of this tractor shed chasing a lizard. It was so fast. That lizard got caught pretty quick.' Garnet Draper shifted her chair and spread out her brown velveteen skirt. She was quiet spoken and still smiled and laughed in the way of a shy young girl.

Nathan stayed chatting while I wandered along the lower slopes of the canyon cliff behind the cabin. Yuccas and prickly pear cactus shared the dry scree with juniper and piñon. Sage perfumed the burning air as I clipped the leaves underfoot and at the lowest point of the rock fall a silver willow gave sanctuary to a pair of hummingbirds hardly bigger than large moths.

I looked up the canyon to the north and saw another earth-roofed hogan standing in a clearing among cottonwoods and bull-grass. Twisted and long weathered pole shelters flanked the brown hogan and from these a grove of cottonwoods formed an oasis on the west bank of the wash. Their shade stretched, bordering the Drapers' cabin and fences.

'A long time ago when those trees were only three or four feet high it was a much bigger area of trees – but the wash flooded bad and it came right over there and washed about a third of them away.' Garnet had indicated the grove over the fence when I returned from my walk.

'That's our old hand baler in those trees, we don't use that no more. Your son's down by the wash, he's O.K.'

Towering above the corner of the canyon the cliff of pink-orange sandstone seemed almost vertical, its texture and luminosity artificial against the pure blue sky at its rim. From that awe-inspiring edge old Henry Draper had once thrown pine poles down into the canyon for firewood. Falling from those heights the poles shattered upon impact into hundreds of pieces and these were collected and stored for the colder evenings of the fall when the fruit was harvested. A day before this Francis had shown me a photograph of his father, with a team of horses and wagon load of poles on the rim preparing to throw the timber into the canyon.

Around a wedge of rock in a large box canyon a trail led up to the canyon rim and it was this that Henry and his family had used in the old days to visit their fields. In those times they carried water from the spring on the canyon bottom to their hogan on the mesa.

Garnet waved towards the trail. 'He's eighty-four years now – he still walks up and down that trail.'

Sheep and goats came over the rise along the path towards the cottonwoods. Three Navajo boys were herding on foot, two carrying lariats which they swung lazily at the trotting animals.

One bunch had split away from the flock and were bleating along the inside of the Draper fence. Garnet stood half in and half out of the cabin door and threw a few stern remarks at the goats and sheep as they hurriedly found the open gate and joined the flock moving through the tree shadows to the wash.

'I was born way over there. Yes, in a hogan over there.' Garnet Draper pointed to the east side of the canyon. 'Henry's not so good. He has bad headaches.'

The old man lay on the ground at the other side of the big cottonwood.

'In 1900 I was born here in the canyon and my husband down there in 1885.' She pointed this time across the fields to the southeast side of Canyon del Muerto.

Coffee was made in an old smoke blackened kettle over an open fire and then after another short rest Henry and I loaded the hay bales on to the pick-up and we swayed back down the canyon.

Henry drove with his usual rugged style, and at eighty-four he could well be excused for missing the odd gear now and again. Nathan rode with me on top of the alfalfa like a rodeo star until the truck hit a sharp bank at speed and four bales flew off the back as the holding wires snapped. After that we hung on even tighter and nine miles later we crossed the last broad expanse of wash and came out of the canyon. There, from the road running along the mesa we could see in all directions for sixty miles or more.

It was evening and Garnet sat on a rock feeling tired and unwell.

'When I was seventeen [1917] I caught diphtheria and nearly died at Fort Defiance. I was in hospital for five-and-a-half months.

'A lot of people caught a bad flu around that time. They told me I would have to be very careful after that.'

It was time for the last chores of the day and she had just watered the goats down by the horse corral. Like children, the animals sensed the time of day and rang their bells in enthusiastic play.

Garnet got up stiffly and we walked up the slope towards the house. She paused as the dogs rushed out to check my scent.

'I had nine children and we lived in a hogan on the other side of the hill then and all the children, they look after things. They herd the sheep and chop wood and things like that.

'I wanted to go to California but the doctors said I would be brought back in a pine box. So I stay here and end up in a pine box anyway! My children, they are all on the reservation.'

'They all seem to be doing very well,' I said.

'Yes, peoples ask me how they get on so well. What did I do to them when they was little? I told them, when they was growing up there was no Squaw Dances, no wine and drinking beer like now. No rodeos, they just worked – behaved themselves.'

A young rooster gave out a startling mistimed and inexperienced crow ending with a gurgling cough.

'That stupid bird doesn't know what to do.' Garnet turned to the darkened porch and called goodnight as I walked up to the bluff.

Living on the mesa was sometimes hard. It was hot and dusty with the afternoon winds pushing the fine soil into everything. Sleeping bags were daily covered in pink powder film and even well-covered food became gritty. In the evenings I cooked our main meal, mostly canned meat and vegetables with fresh fruit. Powdered milk became monotonous, but storing perishable items of food was impossible in the constant high temperatures and we were thirsty most of the time.

Drying winds and the total lack of shade occasionally made us weak and no matter how often I moved the water container into deeper shadows of the truck or tent it was always warm, except first thing in the morning.

In the mornings and at night we were able to keep open the large wall flap on the south side of the tent which, when rolled up, left just a thin mosquito mesh and a freer passage of air. In the mornings before we went off to explore or go to Chinle for water I would sit under the tarpaulin shade at an old folding metal table the Drapers had given me and write up my journal. Nathan would wander off down to the horses or play with the dogs.

It was a strange quiet world on top of the mesa and often Garnet and Henry stayed in their dark rooms during the middle hours of the day. At first, during these early days, I was worried that I found it difficult to make direct approaches to the old couple to ask them the hundreds of questions that I lay awake at night listening to in my head.

They were shy conservative people, I was a stranger – and an Anglo. So great was my concern at not being too forward in my enquiries that I was in danger of making the points of contact too formal. But it was early days and I had a lot to learn about the Navajo, and myself.

Francis arrived after supper one night and talked of his early interest in becoming a medicine man. As a young boy he had quietly observed the role and workings of the hataali, at first quite convinced that this was to be his way. He saw that they had both power and wealth and played a major role in Navajo life. The more he observed the greater seemed the obstacles and requirements to reach such a position.

When I asked Francis how long it would take to undergo full-time training, he replied, 'Maybe two years, if you are very smart. All the pieces of equipment,' he continued, 'are very difficult to make. Just the medicine man's rattle has to be made with very special things.'

He looked down across the corrals to the south. Dark clouds had filled that portion of the sky and were moving north.

'Looks like we get some rain tonight. So – I was sayin' about this rattle. First, the top, the round part holding the rattle. This has to be made from a small piece of hide from near the spine of a buffalo and then sewn up with deer sinew. Then the stick holding the rattle, that must be cedar to protect the persons from lightnings. Around the handle must be some skin from a bear or mountain lion. At the bottom of the handle is some cows' and horses' hair – and on the top of the rattle they stick eagle feathers.'

Francis, now inspired by his own memory, went on, 'These feathers, these eagle feathers, they cannot be taken from a dead bird. That eagle, he has to be alive and those feathers plucked out of him.'

I listened intently as Francis talked on. We sat at the side of his parents' home and beyond the bluff the sinking sun burned the horizon in oranges and magentas.

'That was just one piece of equipment,' he said smiling, his skin the colour of the sunset. 'I think it was too hard for me to do.

'All the plants for medicine have to be collected from all around, sometimes hundreds of miles away. Sometimes they only grow in one place – maybe a mountain way over in New Mexico or up near Utah.

'You have to learn everything, the special medicines, the prayers, the songs. The timing has to be just right, you know – the time, and the words. When you sing for a sick person and you don't sing it absolutely right you have to go away and then come back and sing the words and tune absolutely right.'

'When you were a boy,' I asked, 'did you actually begin the formal training with the hataali?'

'Well, I sort of kept a low profile on that thing because as soon as they know you're interested they make you go along with them all the time. The training would start right then.'

'By that time,' he said impishly, 'I had decided that maybe I should do something else, a little less difficult maybe. But,' he continued, 'those hataali, they get very rich. When the medicine men treat a sick person and he gets well the person's family they give him horses, maybe four or five cows, perhaps forty or fifty dollars in monies – and lots of corn and stuff like that. And that's for one time only.'

We watched the rain clouds moving towards the mesa and I felt the wind coming. Bits of paper flew across the yard.

'How you guys doing up there? Not too much shade now since we cleared all this land. Used to be lots of rattle-snakes up here but now you don't see them. The gophers, those prairie dogs, there's still plenty of them still. We wanted to poison them but the Navajo Tribal Government say no animal or bird is to be poisoned on the reservation. One day I shot twenty-six, next day fifteen. Now they are too clever, they stay down in their hole.'

Francis left just as the underlit belly of the cloud mass spewed out forked lightning. During July and August showers and thunderstorms are usual in the southwest although as yet I only experienced rainfall very briefly around the Grand Canyon on the journey from California. Although we had missed heavy downpours we had seen the effects of sudden summer storms: freshly cut channels in the red earth, green and fresh growth and the mesas and canyon floors with moist pans of chocolate mud beginning to crack and peel like a rhino's skin under the sun.

Again I felt the fresh wind coming and realised that in our exposed site it might be difficult to hold down the already impatiently flapping tent. Hurriedly I tightened all the corner ropes and tied extra lengths of wire from the outer metal tent frame to additional pegs. Intervals between the lightning flashes and the booms of thunder became closer, the wind beginning to pick up the dust. Mushrooming, the tent wrenched in a wild frenzy at the ropes and pegs while Nathan threw himself on the tent floor in an effort to stop it flying away.

As fast as possible I slewed the truck across the windward end of the tent and hoped its bulk would break the full impending force. There was little else we could do and we fell on to our sleeping-bags and waited for the full impact of the storm.

We waited, tense, imagining the yellow tent blown in ragged pieces across the mesa.

Nothing happened, although the wind continued to barrage the bluff, rain had not fallen. I got up and went outside. Slightly veering east the storm cloud had passed over Chinle to the south and the previously tightly stretched leaden clouds were now torn. Flimsy edged sheets of rain were to drench the lower land, perhaps cutting across the mouth of the canyon. Slowly, the harassing wind died and a new moon with its million attendant stars brought a clear beautiful night. Somewhere else it would be deep chocolate mud.

We breakfasted next morning to the usual accompaniment of the bells of Henry Draper's goats and then drove forty miles south to Hubbells Trading Post at Ganado. Juan Lorenzo Hubbell, a trader of Mexican and Anglo parentage, gave this trading post, perhaps the most famous in the southwest, its name. Hubbell established a vast trading empire through the great tracts of Indian country of Arizona and New Mexico and from about 1878 built up this major trading centre at Ganado, meaning 'herd of cattle' in Spanish. It was he who had encouraged the development of high quality weaving among the

Navajo and even went so far as to produce a mail-order catalogue that was sent to potential buyers in the eastern states.

By the standards of the time the household and business were elaborate – their honesty and hospitality famous. Don Lorenzo was more or less a king with a business empire and was visited by notable travellers and at least two presidents were among the well-informed guests who had dined with him and his family.

Until quite recently the ownership of the trading post remained in the Hubbell family. Now it is administered by the National Parks Service and continues to function along its original lines as well as a historic site visited by tourists. It sells much of the merchandise the Indians came to buy and trade for ever since the eighteen-hundreds: flour, salt, sugar and canned goods, together with all the consumer-packaged goods now available to most of American society. Raw wool and rugs are traded by the Navajos of the area, the most prominent rug style being the so-called Ganado Red.

Corrals, barns and storehouses from the early days are still there alongside the rambling Hubbell house full of fine Navajo rugs, Papago and Pima Indian baskets. Drawings, paintings and photographs of Indians from many tribes across the great plains and south-west cover the walls but it was the extreme south-west Navajo area that Juan Lorenzo Hubbell loved most.

By repute he was a fair and honest intermediary between the Navajo and the encroaching Anglo world – and, unlike many other traders and Indian agents who became corrupt or desperately inefficient, Hubbell retained the respect and loyalty of his Indian neighbours.

Remote even today, the trading post was not easily accessible until the 1960s when a paved highway was built from Ganado to the busy town of Gallup across the border in New Mexico. Even with this convenience the last winter had been unusually wet and road conditions so bad in outlying areas where only dirt roads exist, that planes were used to fly in supplies for people and animals. Even with four-wheel drive the ubiquitous pick-up trucks were totally inadequate for the appalling conditions created by the mud and water.

Experts consider that the Navajo weavers have reached the highest quality in their craft so far and many rugs are sold long before they have been completed and taken from the loom. Deliberating a long time I finally bought a small rug by a weaver of Nazlini, a district between Chinle and Ganado. Our limited finance decided its size but not the great pleasure I felt as I carried my prize from Hubbells Trading Post. Nazlini and Chinle weavers use only natural and vegetable dyes whereas the women of some areas of the Navajo Reservation tend to obtain their colours from aniline chemical dyes. The Ganado Red, as its name implies, relies on a strong ruby red aniline dye with associate black, grey and white for a monochrome enhancing contrast.

Trading posts remain important and interesting focal points of Navajo life. Spread throughout the length and breadth of the reservation they, like Hubbells, fulfil a traditional social and economic role. People come in from their scattered and remote hogans to buy and trade for the essentials of life, goods that will keep without refrigeration. More often than not the posts are quite solitary or are set apart from small Navajo communities that may have sprung up comparatively recently. The trading post offers the chance of watching others and meeting distant relatives and clan members and because it attracts fair-sized groups of people at intervals, particularly on the days that welfare cheques are received, it sometimes becomes a stage for anxiety, high emotion and often drama.

Liquor obtained from local bootleggers by young as well as old, often affects the mood around the trading post. At Garcia's Trading Post in Chinle the week before, one fellow had his throat cut and although not a common occurrence, emotions held back when sober can burst forth suddenly with the aid of whisky. A long-felt dislike for one person or another, an accusation or suspicion of witchcraft, sometimes jealousy or envy, innuendoes towards another man's wife or girl friend can cause a fight. Navajos, especially the men, seldom show humour or a sense of well-being when drunk and like some groups in Anglo society, they become morose and aggressive. Many detailed and extensive studies have been made of Indian drinking habits and attitudes. Some believe that their behaviour is the result of cultural erosion and extreme anxiety often contained within a subconscious awareness. Other theories and analysis points to a form of extravagant display linked to representation of a form of equality with Anglo society. Generally, however, the trading post affords positive opportunities rather than negative.

After a long ride we reached Upper Greasewood Trading Post thirty miles north of Chinle and saw a less glamorous but equally interesting example of Indian trading. Every possible item required by Navajo families in their lonely locations across the mountains and deserts could be obtained in its magic interior. Although pick-up trucks were not for sale – tyres were, right alongside axes, horse bridles and bits. Boots and enormous Indian stetsons, straw and felt with flamboyant braided crown-bands, feathers and buckles lined shelves down one side of the store. Navajo hats today seem to favour a very high crown and well-curved wide brim but a number of men wear the extra high uncreased black felt hats with wide flat brims. These almost classic early store-Indian hats are often decorated with a turquoise set or beaded crown-band and occasionally sport a large single wing feather.

Small pot-bellied cast-iron stoves sat together with boots and shirts. In a small side-room were a number of rugs woven by local Navajo women in the Lukachukai style called a Yei rug. These rugs usually depict a row of the Navajo ceremonial dancers called Yeis with a surrounding solitary heavy border. Aniline dyes are used for colours while backgrounds are of black, white and brown homespun yarn.

In the centre of the store were the main food counters and here Navajo women congregated in quiet groups. All wore velveteen skirts and blouses of dark purples and greens. Their hair was tied in the traditional knot with a binding of white wool and upon their wrists were heavy bracelets of silver and turquoise.

A few men fingered the hardware, looking at the axes first and then wandering down to the other end where the saddles hung. Outside were gasoline pumps and several small cabins at the side of large log-constructed barns and storehouses. Beyond these, dotted among the piñon were a number of hogans and then the abrupt height of the Chuska Mountains.

Quietly the Navajos went about their trading at the foot of the mountains, the children running off into the juniper to where a woman sat weaving in the afternoon sun.

Nathan guzzled his Coke and I washed away red dust with a quart of orange juice. Drinking warm water from a plastic five-gallon container made our thirst for cold drinks insatiable up on the mesa. At trading posts when the opportunity arose we consumed almost any cold liquid; chocolate milk became our idea of heaven.

As the days went by I felt more sure of our acceptance by the old couple. Our relationship was developing naturally. Certainly there were times when Garnet and Henry had viewed our presence with some amusement but at least it was not indifference.

As we were unlikely to make much of a move towards deliberate daily occasions of communication, we came in contact at odd times and with ease.

Nathan of course talked to Garnet a lot in the course of his wanderings down to the stock pens and in his play with the dogs. Often I heard the old lady laugh at his antics and the strangeness of his accent. It was obvious that through him we were being gradually assimilated into the family in a simple father and son role rather than me being identified solely as an Anglo who, for unfathomable reasons, had wanted to live with The People.

In the mornings Henry would let the goats out and then go up to the windmill to check the water tank.

'Ho, you O.K. up here?' he called from the truck as he stopped at the loose wire gate. 'Lot a sun eh? Francis, he come over tonight maybe. I go up to check the cattle, we have the branding in a few days now.'

I began to understand that Francis was pleased with my genuine interest in The People and his family in particular and that he had more or less assumed responsibility for my initial period of introduction. Henry and Garnet, it seemed, recognized this and often assured me in their subtle way that I had not been forgotten.

Henry slaughtered a sheep one morning and towards noon Garnet cooked the animal on an open fire in preparation for visitors later that day. While writing beneath the shade of the rough tarpaulin shelter attached to the tent Nathan appeared with a plateful of roasted ribs sent up by the old lady. Small tokens of concern such as this occurred from time to time and it became clear that our presence was not merely a matter of polite acceptance.

As his father had predicted, Francis arrived later and invited me to go down with him into the canyon. He was to cut alfalfa for his mother-in-law at Standing Cow. This entry into the canyon was to be on foot by the steep trail starting at the rim about two miles from Henry's ranch.

Of course I jumped at the chance of taking a new route to the canyon floor and rode with Francis through the piñon and juniper to the rim. At about six o'clock that evening we began the descent at the head of the V-shaped side canyon that opened into the main Canyon del Muerto. Much of the trail and walls of the canyon to our right and left were in rich purple shadow as we followed the Indian path down and due east.

Navajos had used the trail for centuries, bringing sheep, goats and horses down to the spring and summer grasses. Loose rock and shale were in places held by poles laid lengthways across the narrow trail while along other stretches the rock had been hacked into rough steps.

Ahead of us, the eastern rim of the canyon proper was brilliantly illuminated to a depth of about fifty feet by a band of gold. Below that softer browns, ochres and pinks still appeared to exude light captured during the main heat of the day. We zigzagged downwards, Francis leading while I followed briskly stepping from rock to rock, from eroded footholds to sloping furrowed shelves worn by the hooves of Navajo sheep and goats.

An ancient-faced old man came up the trail, his eyes holding the peculiar almost unfocussed look of someone whose life has been spent looking into great distances. His eyes were set deep in a faced lined with years of hardship and acceptance of nature's supremacy in a harsh land.

Francis called out in greeting and the old man cackled and scratched the back of his grizzled head where his red head band was tied. Neither party stopped, one going down, the other coming up from the canyon floor, the laughing banter echoing from the rocks and then the old man and his dogs were gone.

We reached the lower slopes and moved on across the deep sand of a dry rainwater channel. Pointing up to a rock overhang near the base of the canyon wall on our left Francis said, 'You don't see much there no more but that place there is a ruin from the old times. Used to be walls along that ledge but I guess Navajo sheepherders knocked 'em down.

'One time me and my brothers, Bill, Tommy and Richard, were herding sheep and goats when we was boys and the animals wandered up there. They was sort of lying down resting in the shade up there. Well, I climbed up to check 'em out and when I was walking along that ledge I saw some brown hair sticking up out of the sand. I think I was a bit frightened and called my brothers up and we dug around with our hands and we found this body. Well it was all wrapped up and dried out like what they call a Mummy. It was all bent up with its knees up against its chest. There was grass wrapped round the body.

'We was scared so we buried it again, further over, down nearer the other end of that ledge. I don't know exactly where now.'

Reaching the main trail we climbed through the fence at the edge of the Draper's land and came to the giant cottonwood. Francis remembered half-way down the trail that the tractor had a flat tyre; we had continued, half hoping that a pump normally kept at the cabin had not been taken back to the ranch by Henry Draper. A quick inspection of the cabin and tractor shed confirmed the worst and Francis then decided that he would borrow his sister's, Louise Hubbard's, tractor parked at the other side of the field. Here, the small tractor proved to be in good working order but the mower attachment unfortunately seemed faulty. After cutting down a section of the fence separating the two families' holdings we returned to the cabin and hitched Henry Draper's mower to the Hubbard's tractor and drove off down the canyon.

Perched none too securely on a rear wheel cover of the Massey Ferguson I tried hard to keep my balance and listened to Francis's observations as we bounced along the rough trail.

'The Navajo, us Navajo people, we don't seem to think about how to make things better ourselves,' shouted Francis over the engine noise.

That seemed to me a well-meaning over-simplification, especially as all members of the Draper family I had met so far had, to all appearances, considered the future most realistically – and were doing well by most people's standards.

'All these little fields,' he continued, pointing to drier flats above the wash. 'All that land could be irrigated all the time if they dug some wells. Wouldn't have to go down far and they get a lot more crops.'

Concentrating on the conversation and keeping my balance alongside Francis as we pitched and rolled along was a tricky business but my problems were unnoticed and Francis cheerfully shouted further details of his thoughts.

'These Navajo are getting to rely on government welfare payments too much. Things are too easy. They don't think about what they should do themselves. Maybe I shouldn't say that, but it's true.'

Francis shoved hard into a lower gear as we rocked into a narrow section of the wash at the base of a sheer canyon wall. Grinding upwards over the bank and past a row of tarnaric acid willow we entered a shady grove of cottonwoods where a well-constructed hogan stood at the edge of small alfalfa fields.

We were about ten feet above the wash and the field spread from the hogan about sixty yards to the foot of the canyon wall. Running parallel to the trail the field was nearly a hundred yards in length and joined another smaller piece of land to the south. At the north end was another log hogan built right up against the cliff, its back wall formed by the living rock. A small square window looked out to the wash and to the side of the east-facing door was an old weaving frame constructed of two pole uprights set about six feet apart and connected along the top by a single cross piece. To the left of the hogan and probably near fifteen feet above ground on the cliff face was the whitish painting of a horned beast. This was the place called Standing Cow.

Between the hogan belonging to Ella Draper's mother and a stone-and-earth domed bread-oven standing four feet high and approximately four feet in diameter was a bench table covered in food and drink. Seated at this were half a dozen children, a sister of Ella Draper's and the elderly couple who owned the land.

The hogan belonging to Ella Draper's parents at Standing Cow, in the Canyon del Muerto

While her parents and relations quietly ate their meal, Ella Draper bounced her son upon an old bed outside the hogan.

For a while I squatted by the hogan door talking to Ella while Francis took the first cut of alfalfa and then after a cup of coffee I walked across to the rock painting. Standing beneath the Standing Cow I looked across the canyon which at this point was only about a hundred and fifty yards wide before quickly expanding both to the north and south.

Four black horses burst from the willows and galloped along the south boundary of the field. Having, it seemed, escaped from their own pasture further down the canyon, the horses were excited and further confused by the children who now ran to head them off from the alfalfa. Now yelling and laughing the young Navajos were quickly followed by the pack of family dogs whose barking joined their own wild chorus. Abrupt shouts in deeper tones from the old couple further increased the horses' alarm whose squeals pierced all other cries.

I stood transfixed. All sounds were ricocheting from the canyon walls, the echoing noise multiplied into a crashing climax. Each voice, human and animal, rose to the towering walls of rock and reached a piercing crescendo of sound that the canyon itself seemed to emit. It was a haunting cry as though of ancient peoples, of the Anazazi and the Navajo. My ears rang and I saw everything.

First came the Spaniards, then the Utes and Apache, after them the arms of the United States. Anguish, defiance and even joy were locked within the cry rattling from the red rock. Navajos had fought for and defended their canyons stubbornly until even this symbolic heart of their nation felt the equally persistent force of the encroaching Anglo. Kit Carson harried The People through the long winter of 1864 destroying crops and hogans, even the beloved peach trees were hacked to the ground. Starvation and the threat of further military actions broke the spirit of the bewildered and suffering Navajo and they gave themselves up to confinement and indignity.

In the discussions between Barboncito, a senior leader of the Navajo, and General Sherman at Fort Sumner in 1868, which led to the signing of a peace treaty between the Navajo tribe and the United States, Barboncito said, when he understood that the Navajo would be free to return to their homelands after four years of enforced relocation, 'I will take all the Navajos to Cañon de Chelly, leave my family there – taking the rest and scattering them between San Mateo Mountain and San Juan River. I said yesterday this was the heart of the Navajo country.'

A little further on in their talk Barboncito went on to show his great hope and optimism for The People's future.

'After we get back to our country it will brighten up again and the Navajos will be as happy as the land, black clouds will rise and there will be plenty of rain. Corn will grow in abundance and everything look happy.'

Of the nine thousand Navajos confined at Bosque Redondo

in an arid, treeless, flat land, two thousand died during the four years through dysentery, pneumonia and the raids of their enemies, the Comanche.

Quiet fell as the horses withdrew and the children and adults resumed their seats near the hogan. Francis was making his fourth swathe when the mower hit a small rock and one of the triangular cutting blades snapped in half. While he tried humorously to conceal his annoyance at the accident the others peered at the machine and offered unenthusiastic advice. For Francis it had been a string of unlucky events, from the flat tyre to the broken blade. We joked about it being one of those days and he said, grinning widely, 'Yeh, it's one of those days. Me, I have lots of those days – long time now.'

As we drove back towards the Draper's cabin Francis showed me other features of Canyon del Muerto. Hidden trails, almost indistinguishable from the shadows and grooves across giant screes of rock and fissures leading to the rim, were pointed out far above us. As the moon rose, a first quarter of silver against the darkening blue sky, the canyon rim quickly lost its golden edge.

As we passed along the base of the last cliff before the mouth of the rim trail canyon Francis indicated a large pattern of manganese and oxide stains on the rock face above us.

'All sorts of things you can see up there if you look carefully. See that big long mark there? That's a Navajo lady with a turtle in her outstretched hands and see – way over there to the left – that's a coyote on its back with its long pointed ears and tail sticking out.

'If you go over there to the other side of the canyon early in the morning you can see many different peoples and animals up there on the rock.

'Look, see that?' Francis, driving the tractor with one hand over a large lump of rock, pointed across to another dark shape. 'That's a lady with her hair tied up in the Navajo knot at the back of her head – and next to her is a big crow with its wings stretched way out.'

As I looked at the cliff face it offered up more and more images. Some patches of darker rock stood out in relief and had been etched and chiselled by countless years of frost and seeping winter rains.

'These are like faces in the clouds,' he said and then pointing to the other side of the canyon, 'See that big crack like a snake? The People say that was done by lightning, there's a lot of superstition about that.'

Great slabs of stone with clean cut and precise rectangular shapes hung out above the trail, poised as though about to release their hold and crash down upon us. I indicated one that we were passing beneath and remarked that it surely must fall soon. Francis looked up and said quite seriously, 'Maybe it falls right now.'

We began the walk back to the canyon rim. Now that the sun had gone, we had to step carefully on the steep path and although the fierce heat of day had passed we soon felt the effects of the climb and had to pause every few hundred feet to catch our breath.

When young, Francis and his brothers had raced up and down this track for the sheer joy of running when herding the sheep and goats. Such had been their skill and endurance that they, like other Navajos, had achieved honours in state athletic track events.

Moonlight enhanced the rocks and canyon walls perhaps even more than the sun. Its gleaming effects evoked mystery even upon the shadowy rampart of rock that overhung the place where Francis had discovered the Anazazi burial.

Looking back down the trail into the darkness, Francis stopped and listened. 'A man is riding up the trail.' I strained my ears but could hear nothing, and when I turned Francis had gone into the rocks.

In the darkness a little before dawn a string of horses swept down over the bluff from the north section of the range. I heard the hoofbeats sometime before the animals arrived as I lay in my sleeping-bag feeling the sound through the earth. At first I suspected the cattle had taken it into their heads to stampede but the distinctive sound of horses' hoofs soon became obvious. At a run the mares had passed on either side of the tent and then stopped abruptly at the fence by the hogan. Through the tent fly screen I could just make out the silhouette of one horse against a faintly paling eastern horizon.

Wheeling, the horse walked out of sight snorting deeply. I could hear others nearer, on the other side of the tent. Fearing that the excited animals might tangle themselves in the guy ropes I shouted out at them and heard them suddenly shy away and gallop off across the mesa to the west.

From my own knowledge the Draper's horses were always corralled or kept in a fenced pasture further over towards the canyon rim and when I compared the image of the horse by the fence and those of the ranch it had seemed less well bred.

Shortly after the first greyness of dawn, lights appeared along the track from the road and a pick-up truck pulled up at the yard gate. A stetsoned figure got out and walked out into the pasture near the tent. Looking intently at the soft dry earth the man began to cast around in a semicircle and then found the horse's tracks. He followed them for a short distance while I watched from the darkness of the tent, and then apparently confident as to their direction of flight, got back into the truck and drove away.

When the sun was fully above the horizon Francis and another rider came. It was the day of the branding.

Goat bells sounded like a call to school and we got up while the two riders moved across the bluff and returned a little later with the small Draper herd. We were dressed by the time the bawling steers passed through the yard gate and down the hill to the road.

Two miles away at the corrals belonging to the people of the Del Muerto area the cattle were to be branded and vaccinated. At this time of the year calves and horses are branded, ear-punched and immunised against disease. Tribal officials inspect and record the stock numbers being bred and kept in all the areas of the reservation. Such an event brings together the scattered members of the community in an enjoyable social and business occasion.

Nathan proudly wore his western straw hat in the company of the young Navajo boys hung out of the cab window as we edged past the groups of cattle and riders emerging from the piñon and juniper along the mesa top. We arrived at the collection of sun-bleached corrals opposite the Presbyterian Church of Del Muerto. It was here that the grizzly bear skin

An old hogan nestling beneath the wall of Canyon del Muerto at
Standing Cow

had hung for many years and the church to which Garnet and Henry Draper belonged.

Pick-up trucks and small stock trailers were already parked around the enclosures and clustered in groups. Navajos talked and waited for the first animals.

Alert and bawling, the Draper animals were driven into the wooden pole corral where disliking their sudden confinement they stirred the dust into a thick cloud. More of The People arrived, the horsemen coming through the trees and the trucks turning in from the road as the sun rose higher into a cloudless morning sky.

A pit was quickly dug outside the main corral and a fire of juniper logs made to heat the branding irons. Each stock owner brought irons to the fire when his own cattle were ready and there a man supervised their heating and calculated their readiness when called for from the corral. Roping and the holding of stock was, for the most part, carried out by a team of five young men. One was responsible for injections, another for castration while the others did the general manhandling of the unbranded animals.

Mature branded cattle had been herded in with their calves and when separated they were almost impossible to control. Irons were called for and the first calf was roped and dragged close to the fence. Hats flew off, men tripped and sprawled in the dust laughing at their own clumsiness.

One rope stretched out from the tied forelegs and another from the hindlegs, a youth straining at either end. Holding the head and animal's flanks tightly down were two or three others. Francis Draper took the first red-hot iron through the corral fence and carefully positioned the first of three letters on the animal's upper flank. The calf bawled as the iron burnt through hair and into the hide, the smell of scorched hair mingling with the dust of the milling herd in the far corner of the corral. Heads lowered, some with large curved horns, the cows seemed to sense or remember their own ordeal when calves and called out in sympathy to their young.

Second and third irons were applied and the injection given. Francis shouted with achievement and the calf, suddenly released, flapped its ears in surprise and then gambolled away to join its mother. Excitement among animals and Navajos grew

At the branding at Del Muerto

Francis Draper brands a calf

as the branding progressed with the calf-catchers falling and yelling as the beasts bucked and twisted away from the ropes. From the upper rails of the corral the onlookers shouted encouragement or good-humoured insults, and others stuck their grinning faces through the lower rails.

During a lull following the Draper branding and before the arrival of the next group of animals, a black-hatted young Navajo, his red shirt sweat-stained and flapping in disorder, came over to ask where I was from. I told him and he went on to say that he and the other four had started branding on a mesa some way off to the south-east, a place called White Cliffs.

'We started up there and now we are here, today and tomorrow maybe. Then on Monday we go down to Valley Store over near Many Farms.'

Spitting into the dust the Indian cowboy wiped the inside band of his hat. 'It's better than doin' nothin'. We get paid by the day.'

He yelled in Navajo at the rest of the team squatting along the fence and they strolled across to the Draper's trucks and trailers. After each session of branding the owners offered the team food and drink and now they consumed watermelon, cold drinks and savouries with almost as much enthusiasm as they displayed in the corral.

Quite soon the new herd arrived and the cowboys picked up their ropes and returned once more to work. Dust flicked out in spurts between the rails and wafted in clouds over the nervous animals and men. Slithering and straining against the taut ropes the Indians wrestled the calves, stamped searing brands into their hides and castrated the terrified bull calves. Their eyes rolled back in clamped skulls while grey lolling tongues soaked up the dust.

Razor sharp knives notched ears filled with the dull hammering of hooves and the cries of men whose lives had always been linked with those of the animals. The sudden pain was gone, a piece of flesh fell and was buried with the blood in the red earth.

A young black mare stood stiff-legged, her eyes wide. Cleared of cattle, the corral framed the single animal with an uncanny dust-free space.

Standing at the side of the mare the tallest Navajo roper held down a black straining ear in each hand. A rope round its neck

Ella Draper's brother biting a horse's ear during the branding

went out to an Indian whose hatband displayed the name
CASEY worked in coloured beads. As the first iron was brought
from the fire the tall Navajo pushed the mare's left ear into his
mouth and bit down hard. The mare remained frozen, her legs
still rigid. Blue grey around the dark of its eyes became more
luminous as the horse's attention riveted on the message of pain
from its ear. At the rump end of its body, on the left hip a red hot
branding iron cut neatly through the shining black hair and
seared the skin. During the time when the three separate irons
were placed against her the black mare did not move. With his
red baseball cap pulled low over his eyes the tall Navajo
released the ear and to the amusement of others spat a great

deal. Stepping high the young black mare threw its head as though in disgust and arrogantly walked away.

Throughout the 25,000 square miles of the Navajo reservation the Indian horse remains a talisman of the past and an unmistakable reminder of The People's times of strength.

Perhaps when the horses no longer hold that past and The People's present esteem their culture will have become irrevocably diluted by the dominant Anglo world. Navajos in many instances keep horses but no longer ride them, the animals often marking a man's rank although he and his family may ride an eight-cylinder Detroit-bred mount.

Across the valley floor giant creased fingers of rock thrust upwards in uncowed abruptness through the shimmering air. Beyond them were fists of stone and red buttes created twenty-five million years ago, slashed by ice and torrents of water which had pushed red rivers through an infant world.

One hundred and forty miles north of Chinle the Volkswagen truck beat its tiny tattoo through the dust and across the exposed skeletons of rock. Like a minute milk-white grub it nibbled at the orange-red earth in its path. Among monolithic stands of tortured stone and wind-raked sage the Navajo of Monument Valley cling to the breast of the earth. Living out their short man-lives they acknowledge the earth's endurance and survive according to its dictates of mood.

To the east of Elephant Butte a hogan's earth-domed roof capped the mint-green sage and then vanished at the next rib of rock. Heat waves sucked up life, rippled the horizon where light and shade fused into softer tones, and a distant horseman seemed to float above the earth.

Escarpments dwarfed our shadows with their own. A raven sailed out from the topmost ledge spotting the land with its shadow, a soaring shaman above the striped shade.

Three hundred yards from the trail was the log hogan. In its meagre shade stood the galvanised water tank that had been filled at Kayenta and hauled thirty miles. In this northernmost section of the reservation the Navajo of Monument Valley are less influenced by the more urban way of transitional centres such as Chinle and Kayenta where the hubs of B.I.A. administration revolve and the inevitable commercial persuasions begin to bite. At places such as these throughout the twenty-five thousand square miles of the Navajo reservation the manipulation of a bureaucratic structure tightens. Tribal government has to stand with a foot in each camp. Federal policies and the conservatism of the The People achieve an often unproductive compromise and the cohesive power of the Navajo is constantly tested.

Twisted silver-grey juniper branches cut years ago supported each other in a low cone, the high sun turning the shadows into the spokes of a wheel. A ghost wind passed through the old sweat house at the base of Rain God Mesa.

Distant bleats of sheep and goats were absorbed by the great space of Monument Valley. No longer did the great flocks of centuries past cover it. Sawing teeth had then chewed and threshed the scant grasses for over a hundred years, eating new growth before the seed had blown away. Overgrazing had removed the tenuous balance holding plant and soil together and when the rains came the soil was washed away. Winds raped the land and broke the last feeble hold of top soil, leaving great areas naked and stripped of grass.

Wealth, from the time of the Long Walk, became increasingly related to the number of sheep a man owned. Unchecked, the flocks grew to alarming size, and in places the land became desert where once it had sustained good seasonal growth. Erosion became a threat which even the Navajo had begun to see but in their unstructured society could not stop its advance – and many refused to recognise the problem.

Flocks had to be reduced and in 1944 the government began a very unpopular programme of stock reduction and land management. Reseeding and erosion control was fairly straightforward but as this was directly linked to the reduction of sheep all aspects of the Federal policy were viewed with alarm by the Navajo.

Even now attitudes are tinged by nostalgia for the old days when the large flocks were a symbol of the tribe's security. But, at last, new crops, irrigation, beef production and experimental farming are beginning to find a foothold, despite the controversy that surrounds many of the agricultural policies.

With all the confusion and pain of cultural conflicts the

A hogan in Monument Valley

Navajo are still of the land, a scarred ancient land which is desperately short of water and one in which the elements are as punishing as they were for prehistoric man.

Above the damp sand of the wash where the solitary horseman squatted beneath a stunted cottonwood a mile to the East of Rain God Mesa was the stem of rock called the Totem Pole. Set apart from a massive sandstone bulk and cracked into a hundred thousand fissures Totem Pole Rock marked the beginning of a desert plain that spreads into blue crumbling warts of stone. Upon the dipping land to the west was the old wagon trail, a skinny thread pulled tight across the sage.

Shifting in its slow arc behind us the sun brought the

hammering heat of afternoon. I turned the truck into its full glare and followed the trail back around the sentinels of rock which stood darker now. We passed three more hogans set back from the trail on higher ground. Lonely red earth people will never let go of their partnership with the land, even though the young might seek their fortunes elsewhere.

We stopped and felt the furnace heat while, gently, the trail dust settled behind us. Nathan lay on the back seat lost in his own world and saturated with the full melodies of a Dr Zhivago cassette tape rising in heroic volume, appropriate to the character of our surroundings.

My eyes searched the land. For something smaller? Less awe-inspiring? It was as if nature had made one of her gestures of intimidation, a reminder of the real scale of time. I could hardly breathe and think at the same time until I let my mind run out freely into the shadows.

What place in the future have The People and what of their language? Surely it must be the schools that feel for the right way. Such a fragile course is fraught with dangerous misconceptions and suspicion on both sides of the Indian and Anglo world.

We returned to the quiet mesa top at Chinle and settled in its simple sweep of yellow grass. Richard Draper's sixteen-year-old daughter, Kim, spoke to me from the saddle of her horse. She had finished practising her barrel racing in preparation for the rodeo at Gallup. Her grandfather, Henry Draper, was driving the goats back from their wanderings near the road.

'We must recognise that it is an Anglo world,' she said. 'We have to be able to do as well as anybody. Many children now cannot speak Navajo, even though their parents speak it. I confess that I am one of those. I can understand quite a lot and speak a bit, but that's all.

'At a school I went to the girls were made to have their long hair cut and we were forbidden to speak Navajo among ourselves. If they caught us speaking Navajo we were in real trouble.

'I'm going to a veterinary school and would like to set up a practice for large animals somewhere in the area of Chinle. A lot of young people drop out of school and sort of don't bother anymore. Unemployment is high but agriculture should be developed much faster. Agricultural techniques really made a lot of youngsters think about our future at school, they really got into that for a while.

'The old people, they think God gave them this land and that they must only take out of it what God put there.'

All notice boards in Chinle proclaim the word of God through the exhortations of a multitude of doctrinal religions. Camp revival meetings vied with the Baptists, Methodists, Presbyterians, Latter Day Saints, members of the True Church of God and Catholic Church. Churches and missions embellished the administrative centres of the reservation as vigorously as cottonwood trees near a half-dry wash. The word of God floods the Navajo world, its spokesmen appealing through an overwhelming variety of methods.

'When I was a boy,' Francis had said, 'every hogan used the medicine man. There were hundreds of medicine men in these parts, now maybe eight just round here.

'My family, we became Presbyterians, maybe we needed help through the church to improve ourselves.'

Many Navajos have found a way through to an Anglo world via its religions. Some like Francis crossed easily from one side to the other while others had become disillusioned with the Anglo concept of religion, and most will always be deeply convinced by the old spiritual world of the Navajo.

Living from day to day close to the Navajo land was having a profound effect upon the way in which I began to understand the viewpoint from which The People saw their relationship to nature. Despite the ever-growing trappings of the outer world the Indians' heritage was still strong enough to provide an instinctive barricade against values of the Anglo world. There are of course cases of instant acceptance through novelty and social prestige; Navajos are as susceptible to brainwashing as their Anglo counterparts.

All the Navajos that I had so far come into contact with, whether traditionally-minded or progressive had positive opinions towards and a shrewd analysis of Anglo society.

'I haven't been weaving this winter or summer.' Garnet Draper stood in the shadow of the house, her voice thin, floating away. 'Something is wrong with my knees. I can't sit down properly to weave.'

Henry, who had been lying on his back on the low porch step with his hat pulled over his face, rolled over and sat up. 'She go to hospital and have operation on her leg. They cut a lump of meat out but they don't find anything. Nothing there.' He was laughing and looked up through the pebble glasses, his head held in its usual quizzical tilt.

'Yes, that's right,' Garnet chipped in. 'I used to be weaving all the time, but not this year. I have all my wool dyed and ready. Maybe soon I will weave again.'

It was evening and the goats had been herded back to the water trough by the corrals. Once again they had run off to the far corner of the south-east pasture where they pushed under the fence and wandered in their grazing along the road. Almost on principle it seemed, the goats made this excursion. About five hundred acres of range extended west from the ranch but the goats always went to the east. Every day the shaggy little animals with their bells ringing soft-toned in the heat, slowly moved out through the grass and sagebrush, dipped from view into the shallow gullies and vanished.

Early evening usually began with the figure of old Henry standing out by the woodpile shading his eyes while he searched the horizon for his goats. Sometimes he would get into the pick-up and drive down the track and along the road where, more often than not, he would find his animals unconcernedly heading south.

Three sheep accompanied the Draper's goats, about twenty in all, and one of these, a large black-coated animal, wore a big red neckerchief. Sheep and goats or occasionally calves were given to children as either short-lived pets or as symbolic and practical beginnings of their own future herd ownership and independence. This animal belonged to Hank, Bill Draper's thirteen-year-old son.

Henry gathered up the goats and sheep and followed them up to the hogan and then he gave them a light supper of alfalfa, all the while talking to them in Navajo.

'I used to weave outside in the old days when I was looking

after the sheep during the summer. We had a lot then. But, everytime I got started it used to rain.' Garnet laughed at her memories and then shouted at the two dogs now barking at a truck lurching up the track towards the yard.

'My daughters, they always used to say when it was hot, "Mother, why don't you start weaving so that it will rain?"'

'Lots of people round here still weave.'

Within the darkening shadows the old lady pointed to the south, to the canyon rim and juniper-covered ridges. 'I weave in the house now. I'm too old to work outside.'

Garnet went in as the truck swung through the gate. It was a neighbour come for hay and he and Henry went up to the hogan where the goats still munched alfalfa. Two or three mischievous animals had climbed on to boxes and were nibbling the new growth from the lower branches of the two juniper trees.

Above the hogan the bluff was vermilion and along its slope the white-faced steers all faced towards Chinle in the south. One cow, far ahead of the herd, bellowed in a mournful call to the memory of her lost calf sold at the branding. For an hour at dusk she called to the lost calf, looking out beyond the house to the valley where the herd had been driven for branding.

Dogs barked again, straight-legged and heads thrown back. Flag-tailed Spot, the older of the two, dashed out to the rise by the tent and let out long growls between the choruses of aggression towards the distant coyotes' howls along the canyon rim.

In the bat-pierced darkness the cows and calves retreated to higher ground and over the orange earth the black stag beetles clipped quickly to the beginning of their day.

Late morning, next day, I walked through the silence to the windmill. Ahead of me to the left, the prairie dogs stood up on their tails and made their warning squeaks. Their burrows, tubes of earth at the centre of upturned saucer mounds, fitted their occupants perfectly. At a range of forty yards the sentries froze, peering over the clumps of grass and brush at my coming. Closer than that, dignified surveillance was abandoned and they scampered away. Giant grasshoppers clicked blindly out of my way. A horned toad sat mesmerized with its prehistoric scaled head and dagger tail stained with the colours of the hills.

Rotating slowly, the windmill's sails took the slight breeze, the steel lathe stem twisted by the heat into a mirage of wriggling silver worms. Against the purples and blue-greens of the Chuska Mountains the belly of the land pulsed.

Every year the Navajos grow in number. Children run everywhere, the old become fewer and land becomes scarcer. Since their return from their exile at Bosque Redondo, Fort Sumner, in 1868, the Navajo nation has continued to grow. It is as though the energy and life blood of the people had been dammed up until the time of their release. The People quickly repopulated the land and re-claimed the sun-seared earth.

Now they must constantly review their population increase. A nation which relies upon its natural resources as the core of its existence must inevitably feel the uncomfortable pressures created by dwindling land availability. Adjustments to these facts are often painful and confusing and tribal initiatives are not always successful. Those policies and projects which do have significant potential for the future of the Navajo nation are often misinterpreted or rejected outright as being unnecessarily cautious or not being biased enough toward the Navajo, or worse, are Anglo-orientated. Other points of view are that various projects will lead to a debasement of Navajo culture or lack an awareness of the contemporary mood of the Navajo's younger generation.

Mineral discoveries and their exploitation within the reservation has and continues to promote controversy. Fifty percent of the United States uranium sources are held by the Navajo nation and extensive deposits of fossil fuels are among other natural assets found on Navajo land. These give the Navajo an increasing voice in Washington and a means to develop badly needed employment opportunities on the reservation.

'These Navajo, some of them just buy themselves a calendar and sit and watch the days pass until the government cheque comes. No work – but they get money and forget the old ways of how to look after themselves. Me, I worry about that,' Francis had once said. 'I'm Navajo too!'

We drove south along the base of the Chuska mountains which form a cloud-puncturing spine along the north-eastern border of Arizona and the north-western flank of New Mexico. Among these sacred mountains are green meadows and substantial forests of fir and pine. Up here the tall Ponderosa pine dwarfs the stunted piñon of the lower drier mesas and its timber is milled and processed in a tribal enterprise at Navajo, a community about thirty miles north of Window Rock. Between Navajo, regarded as the capital of the nation, and Lukachukai, are small lakes which have formed naturally or in the case of Wheatfields Lake have been established by dam construction.

Catching the mountain rain run-off in a beautiful horseshoe basin edged with tree-draped escarpment and shelving meadows, the lake spread a serene sheet of coolness. Blue sage covered the slopes of the lake's farthest shore and in its simplicity we saw a hogan's dome. Caught in the perfect water were the sharp-faced crags, their reflection hardly discernible from their stark reality. It was the first real water we had seen since leaving California and its effect was marvellous.

Water had become such a luxury to us now. Washing was not an activity that Nathan volunteered for at the best of times and such rationing now, apart from drinking, was for him a somewhat less than difficult economy. Had the heat been that of humid coastal lowlands and not that of high desert dryness our personal scent must have been, in close proximity, interestingly 'natural'.

Refreshing cooler air from the lake washed over us as we lingered and then, following the road, we dropped down towards the state line of New Mexico – our destination the All Indian Ceremonial Rodeo at Gallup.

Sioux buckskins and beaded moccasins in a display cabinet were being intently studied by an Indian in his early twenties. His long hair was braided beneath a tall black hat with its large turkey feather, and he wore a sleeveless singlet, jeans and high-heeled western boots. In his arms he held a baby.

It was difficult to tell from which tribe he came but I had seen his group get out of a truck with British Columbia licence plates. Most probably he belonged to one of the western Canadian tribes, perhaps Blackfoot.

Now a great tradition, the All Indian Ceremonial Gathering

at Gallup is hosted by the Navajo nation and the participants in rodeo, dancing and sports events are from Indian tribes all over North America. Dancing and singing must in some ways help to foster a greater awareness between the various tribes, particularly among the younger, less traditionally aware generation of Indians. Pan-Indianism is, however, a fairly strong movement across North America now and several groups are systematically promoting Indian political and cultural solidarity.

Arts and crafts have a prominent place at this four-day gathering and, although I felt that the marketing of rugs and Indian jewellery was over-managed by non-Indian dealers, the quality of both these crafts had reached an exceptionally high standard. Turquoise and silver jewellery by Navajo and Zuni silversmiths was, by its quantity and quality, an astonishing display of creativity. Weaving of the finest craftswomen from all parts of the Navajo reservation was stacked in piles and draped everywhere, together with Hopi kachinas and Pueblo pottery.

Competition among the craftsmen and retailers was high. As at every Gallup 'Ceremonial' the exhibits had been judged by experts and awards made to the best of every craft with the resulting certificates prominently displayed. Wholesale and retail dealers of Indian arts and crafts assemble here from all over the United States and prices are notably not cheap.

Silver and turquoise is as much a feature of Navajo expression as the horse, hogan and sheep. Its daily presentation is commonplace and almost all Navajos have and wear at least one major piece of jewellery. Many of the older generation wear large bracelets, brooches and multipiece belts made of heavy silver and inlaid with turquoise.

Men often wear ketohs, the wide silver and turquoise bracelets, and watchstraps now follow a similar pattern. Older men especially, when visiting civic offices, hospital or local meetings of one kind or another, often display extraordinary amounts of these precious materials which are worn with impressive dignity. Women, through whom come all inherited wealth and clan lineage, are more exotically bedecked on special occasions. But even for a family visit to a coin-operated laundry, they are frequently seen wearing enormous brooches, fine earrings, necklaces, rings and belts made of turquoise and silver.

Being seen so much and worn in a natural and unostentatious manner it is easy to forget just how much the jewellery is worth. Many of the pieces are family heirlooms and may be very old, the inherent value of silver and turquoise seen as a sound and negotiable investment. This of course is outside the jewellery's obvious historic and artistic value so much now appreciated and sought after by Anglo collectors.

Families or individuals experiencing hard times will often pawn these cherished possessions at one of the trading posts and receive credit for goods needed at the time. Perhaps years later, when household or personal finances have improved, the items will be redeemed. Some, however, are left in pawn and these, if not claimed by relatives, are sold.

Established in the earliest days of the trading post enterprises, the system of pawn goods continues today throughout the reservation and is often an essential means of obtaining instant credit. Many very valuable pieces of Navajo jewellery are in other instances deposited with pawn dealers purely for the security they provide. Such owners prefer to pay the monthly interest charges against the silver and turquoise kept safe in the dealer's vault.

Large multi-stone bracelets, brooches and belts are worth usually between a thousand and three thousand dollars and to see some of these personal adornments hanging from a wrist flopped casually over the side of a mud-covered pick-up is not an uncommon sight.

'Welcome to this wonderful Red Rock Park Rodeo arena, folks, on this wonderful afternoon. We're sure glad you made it and we're gonna do our best to make sure you don't leave without havin' a real good time.'

From the air-conditioned and muted light of the Ceremonial Centre's exhibition rooms we stepped out into the glare of the rodeo arena terraces and took our seats for the first events. On the far side of the arena a public address system tower, itself dwarfed by the mountain of smooth red rock which created the natural amphitheatre in which we sat, amplified the rodeo announcer and general compère for the afternoon's events.

Booming out from the tower and the rock face 'the voice' took control.

'Now, I'd like you all to stand and pray with me.'

We all rose up in meek compliance.

'Lord, we hope you'll bless this rodeo and all these fine young people who are goin' to entertain our visitors. We don't ask that the bulls and horses are slow, we don't ask that the rope never fails to find the calf's head or feet. We just want you to bless and guide our spirits and maybe when we reach that big corral in the sky that there will be room enough for all of us. Amen.

'Now folks, remain standing while we play that greatest song in the world – God Bless America.'

Walls of rock towering over the arena reverberated with the anthem and white men took off their cowboy hats and placed their hands on their hearts. They were visibly moved and proud of America even if they were for the moment outnumbered by the Indians.

'We're all Indians out here today folks. Indians from all over and we, the Navajo Nation, welcome you.

'Now, our rodeo contestants are athletes who have trained long and hard at their own expense and by golly, folks, they're a special sort of people. Yes sir! They travel all over, hauling their gear in pick-ups or just hitchin' a ride to the next rodeo with their friends.

'They pay forty dollars each to ride in any event in the hope that they'll pick up some points before finding themselves upside down in nowhere. Yessir, by golly, these are hard workin' folks.'

Dutifully, as instructed, we all sat down and munched our popcorn.

'Isn't it wonderful this afternoon – a sunny ninety-four degrees folks. We're sure gonna have a good time. And here we go. Jimmy Yazzie is gonna ride Flippsy out of chute number three. This is bare back bronc riding and these horses sure know where the sky is. Yessir.

'Whoops. There goes Jimmy, boy he sure is hanging on there. Hey, did I say hanging on? Where are you Jimmy boy?

'Hey, there you are. Bad luck old timer. We'll get that hat for you just as soon as those catchers run down old Flippsy.

'That horse is really somethin', isn't he folks?'

We all agreed with that, somewhat surprised the rider was still alive.

'Hey, and here's those big bulls. Boy, are they mean!'

Settling into his position of authority and shaded seat the anonymous Navajo fairly rattled with enthusiasm while the crowd became moist on its rear end in a 'wonderful sunny ninety-four degrees.'

'This fella is really mean. He's called Adio and here he comes out of gate seven ridden by Henry Bigman out of my home town Round Rock. Look at that Brahma bull go. That's it, one hand only Henry. Look out Henry, he's after your trailer hitch with those horns. Bad luck Henry. Boy, that must have hurt. Help him out of there.

'Give him a round of applause you wonderful people. He just spent forty dollars to get thrown off like that. Better luck next time, Henry.

'What a mean one. Why he's as mean as my wife! Why, she's so mean she goes bear huntin' with a fly swat. Yessir!

'When these fellas come outa the chute on these saddle broncs they have to spur them high up on the shoulder on the first jump – otherwise they get disqualified. Now folks this is some fine stock you're seein' here this afternoon. These animals have bucked off the finest all over the country.

'Here comes Steve Tso outa number five. Hey, Ay, look at old THUNDERBIRD go. Boy, he's gonna make it – there you go, that's the buzzer.

'Now, get off that wild thing Steve before she busts a gut. That's it fella, look at her kick.'

My back was on fire and the reflected sunlight seared my eyeballs. Two tiny figures appeared above the crowd on the massive shoulders of red rock as we watched Kim Draper compete in the barrel racing.

Navajo girls streaked around a figure-eight course hurling their tough horses around painted oil barrels in a test of speed and skillful manoeuvres. Nathan whooped in encouragement and then leapt over the fence to join a great crowd of children stretched across the arena in a tug of war. With a backside covered in a mixture of horse dung and red earth he then scrambled with the horde of youngsters in a race for a prize of fruit. Oranges, melons and apples flew in all directions and those not flattened beneath the squirming bodies were carried triumphantly back to their parents. Grinning widely, Nathan

An old Plains Indian woman drinks a Coke and contemplates, at the All Indian Ceremonial at Gallup, New Mexico

returned with a gritty armful of oranges and we sucked out their juice.

The Navajo announcer cut through the heat again. 'Before we go into the calf roping, you wonderful people, let's all stand up and get the kinks out of those butts.'

Most of the crowd did as they were told and went through the motions of stretching.

'Did you hear about the Navajo who was standing down on Main Street in Gallup and every time a girl went by he called out to her "Chance". Well this went on all day and finally this fella comes over to the Navajo and says, "Hey, Chief, how come you don't say 'How' when you speak to those girls? How come you always say 'Chance'?" So this old Navajo fella he looks right back at him and says, "Well, I know 'how', all I want is a 'chance'!"

'Well, by golly, here we go again with some calf roping and steer wrestling.'

Through the blazing heat of the afternoon the enthusiasm of the announcer continued. 'By golly, folks' whipped through the dust and the 'wonderful people' finally left feeling that they had had 'a real good time'.

It was mid-August and the late summer rains fell from a dark sky along the crests of the Chuska Mountains. In one clear moment the earth took in the glassy fusillade of the storm's coming and held its breath. Like grey blue horsetails the curtain smeared the piñon slopes before slicing through the sage and across the backs of the goats.

The earth breathed. From the punctured soil steamed a smell saturated with the ingredients of the earth's beginnings, its fullness almost choking. Out of that pungency came the essence of the land, a secret fertility within its depths.

Beneath the dripping junipers the goat bells sounded faintly, sheathed in hissing wind and the passing rattle of thunder. Snatching at the new growth, never halting, the animals' jaws quickened in the moving patterns of light and dark. Sharp pricking hoofs were stained red and shaggy under-bellies slicked to jagged combs.

On the horizon forty miles to the south were three small but distinct pyramid-shaped hills.

'See those hills way over there? Yes, those little bumps. We live right there. You're welcome to come over and stay in the hogan. You can meet some people there and do whatever you want to do.'

It was dusk. Bill Draper had driven over from Ganado to introduce himself and offer an invitation to join him and his family for a while. Bill had written to me in England assuring me that I would be able to live alongside his parents, Garnet and Henry Draper. Bill was involved with area administration of educational finance in the Bureau of Indian Affairs at Window Rock, and quite a proportion of his time was spent travelling across the reservation. Because of this he had been unable, since my arrival at Chinle, to meet me and find out for himself my real interests in the Navajo.

We stood by the shelter where the sheep meat was hung to dry. Bill was stocky with a broad round face, and wore glasses, a western hat and the obligatory – even for civil servants – pointed cowboy boots.

He was in his late forties and unlike his brother Francis, spoke English with the fluency of early schooling and the experience of further education as a B.I.A. employee and active service in the Korean War. We talked for a while about possible areas of interest to me and the problems facing Navajo education in these present times of Federal cutbacks and the ambitions of the Navajo to control much more of their own educational policies. Bureaucracy within the Navajo nation was no less complex and self-generating as that of Anglo society, often losing sight of original political and social objectives in the maelstrom of departmental self-interest and manoeuvring. Washington could and did make decisions concerning various programmes which, even with all the information available from the B.I.A. on the reservation, occasionally completely ignored the realities of implementation.

It was expected that I would find Bill's home at Ganado and I was not given further directions. It took a long hot morning a couple of days later before I received near final instructions from the Navajo proprietor of Wood Springs Trading Post to reach Bill Draper's hogan.

Three miles east of Ganado I found a road running north to Nazlini and Chinle. We passed a lake and followed the road through a shallow valley running down from the Ganado ridge. On distant slopes and just visible among the juniper and piñon at infrequent intervals were a few hogans but no people. Reaching Wood Springs Trading Post about six miles from the main highway I stopped to ask directions from the owner. A cheerful Navajo told us to go back about a mile and a half before turning west along a track that led to the Draper place.

Three small pointed hills came into view as we drove back the short distance south. On a sweeping crescent ridge sparsely freckled with juniper the three red earth cones Bill Draper had pointed to, two days earlier, forty miles away at Del Muerto, at last signalled the end of our search. Fenced along the road leading up to the house, the pasture at first looked similar to Henry and Garnet's land but it appeared on closer inspection to have been less generously sown.

A bunch of horses picked at the thin grass while up near the trees a herd of goats came out into the sunlight. Chickens scattered in blobs of white as we crossed the fenced yard and pulled up two hundred yards from the cones.

Without any question as to our difficulties in finding the place, Bill welcomed us and introduced his wife, Irene, and the children who happened to be around, about five in all.

A little to the north of the frame house stood the log-walled hogan and this we gladly accepted as our temporary home. It had been made a year or so earlier and was of a stout six-sixed form. Being modern, the roof was of a low-pitched style, made of six elongated wedges of one-inch-thick plywood covered with roofing felt, which, supported by a framework of two-by-fours, coverged to the central chimney hole through which projected the central stove flue.

In the dark interior the earth floor was dry and very dusty; our unpacking and partial rearrangement of the hogan's vast collection of old household furniture and stores created a haze of pink dust.

Puppies, kittens and chickens peered curiously through the east-facing door and then Porky, seven years of age and the youngest of Bill's children, led Nathan away to a conference on the type of games to be played.

Quite suddenly a new phase had begun in our lives and I realised that in their way the family had begun to tell their own story. Events that had affected the Draper's past were part of Navajo history and those happening now and in the future were and would be the general concerns and difficulties of the tribe's ability to hold their own against Anglo domination.

Complex social and cultural pressures continued to cause anxiety and within the extended Draper family all the problems and hopes of the Navajo could be seen clearly from day to day. I felt more and more accepted by the family and having crossed the line as it were from the outside, I began to be able to look back objectively at my own world, at its assumptions about Indian society. Immense cultural problems have been inflicted upon native Indian Americans, often unwittingly, and generated by a belief that 'it's for their own good'. In an age of instant media communication, the Indians, and particularly a large group such as the Navajo, are bombarded with social and materialistic influences which create psychological stress as well as the fashionable phrase 'global awareness'.

Television and radio bring educational opportunities but they also present the sophisticated commercial saturation that implies the inadequate social status of individuals not constantly buying within the consumer market. A quick look around the yard of any Navajo hogan will often reveal a clear picture of status pressure-selling.

From the hogan door I could look down across the shallow valley eastwards. Along the bottom was the paved road and over among the juniper and piñon on the opposite ridges were the scattered dwellings of the Kin Li Chee district. It was a good view, full of space and light, an invitation to let my eye and mind run out across new lands of the reservation.

Bill Draper had begun his life in the traditional Navajo way at Del Muerto. There, along with his brothers and sisters he herded sheep for his father from his infant days. Like all Navajo children he grew up loving the land and recognizing his part in it. He had wandered with the animals over the mesas and had taken them down into the canyon in the spring and summer. All the birds and wild animals he knew. Secret places were sometimes places to play games, sometimes they were the haunts of skinwalkers, the ghosts of the canyons.

Working was living and the sheep and goats were, like the corn, beans and squash, cared for dutifully because they were the strength of the family.

'We took it in turns to look after the sheep and goats, chop wood and all those things. My father and mother assumed, I think – well yes, I'm sure they thought that whatever happened my brothers and sisters would grow up to do the same things they did. We had better damn well know how to herd sheep properly.

'I guess none of us thought too much about things like that but as time went on I sort of felt things were going to be different.'

Bill sat on an upturned bucket by the hogan door one

morning while the sun was still bearable and spoke casually of
his boyhood.

'For some reason my actual birthdate was mixed up and I
don't know why. Some said it was 1934 and others 1932.
Anyway, one day we had been hauling alfalfa, all the family,
and two guys rode up on horses. One was the white government
man and the other a Navajo interpreter.

'They came over to me and said – "How old are you boy?"
And I said that I didn't really know. They said, "Hey boy, put
your arm over your head and get hold of your ear." Well, I was
kinda dumb I guess, and I put my arm over my head and
touched my ear. So this school fella looks at me and says,
"You're old enough – you must go to school."

'Well – I guess my Mom didn't object because pretty soon
after that I was collected along with loads of other kids and
taken to Chinle Boarding School. I don't remember too much
about all that but I remember, I'll always remember, this big
yellow brick wall with all of us kids standing against it under an
orange light. The kids were all crying and carrying on and
making a terrible row, but I don't remember being emotional.
That was how I started school, I was about six years old, it was
1938.'

It took some time to find the right fold of ground along the top
of the mesa. Irene Draper had not been to her dead grandmother's old hogan for about twenty years and she wanted to
show me the old place. I had the feeling that having me along
would be an excuse to check her own memories as well as
explain some of her part of the extended family's history.

We had headed west over the ridge behind the house and had
passed the cluster of hogans and corrals where members of the
'outfit', further relatives and clan associates of Irene's lived
scattered among the juniper.

We tried three trails out through the sagebrush and small
piñon before we found the right area. Irene drove the blue
pick-up along barely visible wagon ruts to where an earthen
mound grew out in an unexpected appendage to the slope of a
gully beginning its way south towards Ganado.

'Even my husband, Bill, hasn't seen this hogan yet. Several
times we've started out but have got sidetracked or been in too
much of a hurry. You should see this because it is underground

and it must be quite unusual.'

In the partial shadows the truck was parked just above and to the east of the hogan, and facing the very small low door. It appeared at first glance more like a weathered earth igloo but as I came nearer the structure became more defined and around the door some of the underlying timber supports were visible.

In form, the hogan was in fact very much like an igloo except that it grew out of the west bank of the gully, the earth of its roof merging into that of the bank.

To pass through the tiny open door I had to crouch, practically crawl, and once inside could only stand straight up at the very centre of the single room dwelling. Cut into the back and south walls were rectangular recesses, these presumably storage shelves for food and utensils. To the left of the door were the remains of the old cooking stove, the chimney still poking up through and above the hogan roof, like a fat black and rusty metal cigar.

An enamel bowl still hung on a nail from a timber roof cross-beam and on the back wall stood a few small tins on wooden box shelves. In diameter the hogan's interior could not have been more than either eight or nine feet wide, the height of the walls four and a half feet and the roof centre perhaps a little under six feet.

'My grandmother used this up to two years before she died. She used to come out here even when she was very old and even after that members of the family herding the sheep out here would eat their midday meal here. See, there's still a can opener here.

'In those days plural marriages were quite common and my grandfather had two wives. My grandmother, she was the second wife and he built this place for her. You can see over there what's left of the old sheep corral – and that little pointed wooden shelter was a storehouse.'

Irene pointed to the structure a few yards away among the sandy mounds below the hogan. Its opening was to the south and was similar in shape to the traditional Navajo sweat house. Beyond this was the overgrown corral, full of sage and patches of prickly pear cactus. On the bank above the hogan lay an old log, its centre chopped out in a V to form a long narrow trough.

Irene Draper's grandmother's underground hogan on the mesa at Ganado. In the doorway is Irene's son Patrick

'That was used for feed and especially salt for the sheep and goats.'

Nathan and Irene's son, Porky, ran in and out of the hogan in play. It was a momentary link through the generations as Patrick, Porky's proper name, the great grandson of the hogan's owner, peered into its dark interior and then inside, peeped out around the door frame, its sagging supports barely tall enough for his seven years to pass through.

Rain clouds were moving up from the south filling the sky with thick soft grey cloud.

'It looks as though it will be a good year for piñon nuts. Last year there was hardly anything – now they're everywhere.'

Seeds from the piñon cones have been a traditional natural food of the Navajo since their beginnings and until recent years were harvested carefully by families all over the mesas where the small pines grow. Now with the convenience of tinned and other packaged foods the Navajo no longer regard the piñon nuts as such an important item of their diet.

'You know in my family some are very pale-skinned and their hair sometimes a little light or wavy. Well my grandmother must have been on very hard times and she got into debt at the trading post, Hubbell's Trading Post down at Ganado. Well, it seems that she had to pay off her debts in other ways to Ramon Hubbell, he was the son of Juan Lorenzo Hubbell, the man that started that trading post. My grandmother, she had a baby for him. That's where some of that light blood comes from.

'I was speaking of plural marriages. They still go on among the Navajo, even today. Of course they can't be declared officially but we know people who live like that. In my family there is an uncle who has maybe three wives – we know for sure of two.'

Irene smiled and then laughed loudly. 'He has twenty-six children at the last count, maybe there's a lot more around. They seem to all get on very well. On pay day he takes his first wife into town to do the shopping while the other wife stays home and looks after the kids.'

Irene took a last look at her grandmother's underground hogan in its hidden gully and then turned the truck and we rumbled back along the old wagon trail. Darker now the clouds hung in twisted cords to the east but the rain still held off.

'In the winter time this red clay is just one big mud puddle. That and the snow makes things near impossible. You can hardly drive up here, and that's with four-wheel drive too! These goats, over there – they're all that's left of my aunt's herd, just a dozen or so sheep.'

Irene looked out across the sage in silence for a few moments and then said quietly, 'I didn't realize there were so few, she used to have a lot.

'We only have three ourselves, two sheep and a goat. They're over at Grandma Draper's. The black one with the red neck-band you saw over there, that's our sheep. My father, he lives up there, in between those two bluffs. You see that house,' Irene said, indicating a small group of buildings half-concealed by trees about a mile to the south. 'I haven't taken you over there because he's a bootlegger, and he's, well, never quite in his right mind. We don't even know where he gets his supplies from but he goes all over to the Squaw Dances selling stuff. The people cuss him out and tell him to go away – they cuss him out all the time. But I guess it makes no difference. Yes, he's quite a guy.

'There's quite a few bootleggers around here, they do all right. One fella runs a place just down by the bridge at Ganado Wash and he's pretty near blind. They call that place Black Cat. The police never get any proof, nobody will testify or anything. With this man maybe The People they consider it's not a bad thing for a disabled person to make a living. The Navajo think like that quite often.'

At the house we met Bill and quickly prepared to visit the mother of Rebecca Martgan, Senior Area Administrator of Navajo Education and based at Window Rock. Rebecca had earlier invited me to meet her elderly mother and now with Bill and Irene to act as go-between we piled into the truck again and headed south.

After seventeen miles from Ganado lies the district of Klagetoh. It is an area of wide sweeping uplands and ridges covered mostly in juniper and piñon. Sage and yellow-flowered snakebush fill any open treeless places, particularly those shallow valleys interrupted by dry water courses and sharply cut gullies.

At the one positive identification of the Klagetoh area, its trading post, we turned west from the paved highway and found the old lady's home a mile or so down a sandy trail.

Most of Rebecca's relatives, her mother, father, and her aunts and uncles, lived a traditional way of life and several of the womenfolk were weavers, including her mother, Mrs Evans. A previous meeting had been arranged that week in which Rebecca herself was to have introduced me to her mother but this had fallen through because of a number of difficulties at Window Rock. Now Bill, an associate and member of the same clan, the Ashinii (the Salt Clan) was to be my interpreter and, knowing the area well, my guide.

A long shade porch with screens overhung the front door of the low frame house and Mrs Evans met us there. She was dressed in the old Navajo style with velveteen blouse and skirt with her hair pulled back in the knot bound with white wool. Her face showed the bone structure from which her daughter had obviously gained her own very attractive features. Shy and gentle, her eyes full of intelligence and reflecting her bright sense of humour and alertness, she led us into her main living-room.

I was curious to see her weaving that Rebecca had mentioned. Both in English and in Navajo she explained that she no longer wove rugs but offered to show me the few she still kept for herself.

'I am too old now and they wanted my loom. You see it's gone. I think they sold it for fifteen dollars,' Mrs Evans smiled in a way that hinted at the irony of such a meaningless price placed upon such personal equipment. 'They' were not explained or referred to again.

By reputation the old lady had been one of the finest Navajo weavers and the various pieces taken out of a large wooden trunk were of the highest quality in both craft and design. Being able to inspect closely such fineness was a privilege and the extreme modesty of the rugs' presentation was an additional pleasure. Many of the rugs made in the past had been exhibited and were now in important private and public collections throughout the United States.

Spreading the rugs, large and small, over the floor and draping them over the furniture, Mrs Evans quietly pointed out the details of her craft.

'Mostly I use vegetable dyes in my weaving, but occasionally commercial dyes; the reds of course are aniline. That pink there is made from cedar roots.

'I have more in that other chest but my daughter must have the key. I just live here in the summer and spring now. In the winter time I stay with Rebecca at Window Rock. It gets too cold here.'

An enormous single beam ran the entire length of the large main room, about twenty-five feet long and about fifteen inches

Rebecca Martgan's mother, Mrs Evans, weaving at her Klagetoh home

square. Supported by the central beam a shallow-pitched roof came down to plastered walls which in places were being resurfaced. A big wood-burning stove took a near central position in the room, its black chimney flue pushing straight up through the boarded roof. At the south end of the room, hanging on the wall above an old madonna-and-child print, was a cradleboard. These infant carriers, very much part of Navajo life, are still used and are usually made of wood and rawhide. A flat board or pair of boards between two feet and three feet long hinged with rawhide form the back of the cradleboard and on to this, wrapped in cloth, the baby is held by a lacing of rawhide thongs. At the base of the cradleboard is a small wooden footboard which supports the child and helps to keep him from slipping down. A deep V-shaped notch is cut into the top of the backboard and this enables the mother to lean the cradleboard against the base of a tree or pole where the baby, in an upright position, can look at his surroundings. Just below the V notch, attached to the backboard and at right angles to it a flat piece of oak or juniper between two and three inches wide forms a half-hoop projecting twelve or eighteen inches to form a safety bar, in the event of the cradleboard falling, or, in summer, a sunshade canopy support.

Nearly all Navajo children have experienced the cradleboard and such is the feeling of security gained from it that many will not go to sleep until placed in their familiar bindings.

Taking a rugged trail we left the house and, directed by the old lady who sat in the cab with Bill and Irene, drove in a westerly direction. Mrs Evans gave me a large quilted winter jacket to wear against the rain which threatened to soak me squatting in the open back of the pick-up.

As soon as we left the main graded trail for an even rougher ride the laden bank of cloud released both rain and thunder split with vivid streaks of lightning. We followed a tortuous series of sunken tracks curving gradually to the south and pushed on through the rain. A slanting downpour hit the silver green sage and then turned the earth to a deepening shade of chocolate before channels of storm water began to cut across our path.

Bill had put the truck into four-wheel drive and clipped along at a fair speed while the thunder shower soaked me to my skin. Through gully bottoms and over sharp ridges the trail wound without any signs of habitation, the red earth soup flying away from the tyres to splatter the clumps of snakebush and multi-leaved yuccas.

Rolling away its dark blanket the storm drifted northwards, its yellow flashes spearing the horizon behind us. Troughs and bends in the trail became increasingly sharper, the way narrower.

Grinding fast from a dip to a sloping crest we came without warning to a small frame cabin and a number of randomly placed outbuildings. A small corral stood off to one side, barely visible beneath a piñon-covered outcrop of shale and earth. Its rails and its real dimensions were mostly hidden by the cracked and peeling trunks of juniper but inside the small space a chestnut mare snorted and cantered in circles.

Mrs Evans entered the cabin first and then an equally shy and soft-spoken elderly woman appeared. She smiled at us and said in Navajo that she had just finished a rug and that it had been removed from the loom. If we wished we were welcome to see it.

A little way from this cabin was another of similar size braced against the rising ground by wooden piles. Its back was to the first cabin, its one door facing east and climbing two or three steps we came into the sister's workroom. Not able to speak English, the old woman spoke in Navajo to Bill and Irene and through them I was able to understand something of the conversation.

Florence Shosi unrolled her rug. It measured about three feet by four, a standard size for most Navajo weaving, and she spread it out for our inspection on a single bed. It was of very good quality and used both natural colours and vegetable dyes. White, black and greys were of undyed wool and soft yellows had been obtained from the Rabbit Bush, the leaves of which are used by the Navajos to make tea. Shade variations in the colours were often the result of the kind of metal container in which the plants were boiled.

Consisting of stripes running across the width of the rug its pattern was relatively simple with those interspersed with three bands of formalised flower shapes. Exquisitely executed the whole effect was one of quiet refinement and obviously reflected the artist's own modest temperament.

As usual I was concerned that we did not impose too much upon these isolated and reserved people. Their modesty and kindness had already shown the quiet dignity with which the Navajo conducted their daily lives and I left feeling yet again more than fortunate at such undemonstrative hospitality.

Hoping to return on another occasion later in the year I said goodbye and with an accompanying feathered display by the family turkeys we climbed into the truck and took the trail back. Unexpectedly, we turned off from the anticipated return route and moving out into what seemed a yet more remote area came to another cabin.

A young woman in her middle or late twenties came to the door and she was introduced by Mrs Evans to us as her sister. In formal Anglo kin relationships she was in fact a niece. Children peeped out from the cabin windows at our arrival and on our entering they scuttled to vantage points around the living-room. The small room in which we stood served as workroom, bedroom and sitting-room and from this a door opened into a larger kitchen and general day living-room.

A large loom stood empty opposite the cabin door and next to it was another small frame showing the beginnings of a new rug. Watched by the children who hid behind furniture like squirrels and her husband smiling and interested in this unexpected visit, the young woman spoke English well, and explained her work and craft methods. Like the children she too was obviously intrigued by our visit, appearing from the grey light of the passing storm and made us feel quickly at ease with her friendly manners.

One batch of dye had gone wrong, she said, and the process must be started again. It was experience, trial and error, the effects of temperature, and quality of both dye plant and wool that often produced unpredictable variations of colour. To control and maintain consistency in dye shades was the problem and universal lot of weavers.

Like Florence Shosi and most Navajo weavers, the young woman took her finished rugs to a trading post and bartered for the best possible price. She would take her new rug to Ganado or perhaps even Gallup when it was finished.

'Sometimes they give me good price at Hubbell's but not always. They make a lot of money out of us down there.'

Picking a little self-consciously at imaginary knots on the surface of the weaving the young woman hushed the children who had now gained a little more confidence and were emerging like gophers with growing squeaks of enthusiasm.

I wondered at their lives out there, a very quiet existence lost among the juniper and mesa gullies. Inside the darkened cabin was an atmosphere of the greatest privacy, timeless, a satellite within a peculiar world, the Navajo world – itself surrounded by a different people.

Suddenly the young mother seemed more a girl, hardly old enough to have such a collection of children. She touched the weaving again as she stood up, as she would a child, reassuring and instinctive. I found her looking at me directly for a moment, her eyes showing interest but also a disquieting feeling that my being there was perhaps, less of a surprise to her than it was to me.

Mrs Evans spoke in Navajo to her niece and the moment was gone. I had an odd sensation of guilt when I said goodbye to the young woman and her husband, such an odd emotion for that place, and as we swung out through the trees leaving the family in its quiet cabin the feeling continued to worry me.

Skirting a wide arroyo cut by the summer flash floods Bill drove on through a shallow valley bordered by piñon-covered ridges. A crow flapped wet black wings in slow flight above the sage. It followed a laconic course – pushed and sucked by the gusting wind. Through the steel-grey space the black bird dropped and rose against the purple belly of the clouds before sinking into the infinite space.

'This is the house of my sister.' Mrs Evans stood for a moment by the truck looking at the cabin before us. It was the colour of the earth. We had driven the last hundred yards through overhanging junipers whose branch tips were silvered with raindrops that fell generously against the truck and then spattered the soil.

Between the trees in front of the solitary cabin the spaces fell into a natural arrangement of small pens and corrals. Rough rails, weathered and twisted, linked live trees in marvellous irregularity. Tree trunks lay horizontally upon stubby timber legs, their upper surfaces crudely hacked out to form feeding troughs. These together with the fence rails presented an unexpected yet harmonious pattern of line beneath wet tangled branches.

With her back to the west facing window sat the old woman. It seemed most likely that she was in her seventies. The two sisters spoke quietly in Navajo together and then looking shyly at me the seated sister smiled. Her manner was gentle with a natural dignity reflecting the character of her life with its simple rhythms. It seemed a face like that of so many Navajo women, to show an acknowledgment of the natural order of their lives within the undisputed authority of their land. It seemed, to me, to show even reverence.

Before the woman was her loom. Half-finished, the rug had absorbed the warmth of a sun lingering among the broken cloud to the west. Our interest in her work caused the old lady some embarrassment and although intrigued with our presence she felt naturally obliged to indicate that her efforts at weaving were worthless.

We told the woman of the rain and how we had come through the storm on our way from Klagetoh. Strangely, she insisted that rain had not fallen on her home, but it was clearly wet outside. Engrossed in the weaving the showers had come and gone, her thoughts uninterrupted.

Her hair was pulled back in the Navajo knot and bound with white woollen yarn. The woman's velveteen blouse was a luminous green and when she crossed the small room to get more wool her long full skirt filled all the space.

Dark and separate, the floor existed as a level far below the woman and the loom. Only the window with its changing mood, the green blouse and the half-finished rug forced the eye to focus. Everything else merged into shadows.

In the cabin doorway the old woman seemed to float in her green blouse when we said goodbye. The two sisters talked while Bill and Irene showed me the old buckboard standing in the juniper shadows. Long elegant shafts rested on the ground, their points buried in a carpet of twigs and bark. Gaunt grey planks scoured along the grain by wind, rain and sand made a million polished ridges and the iron-hooped wheels stood perfectly framed by the ragged informality of their surroundings.

From the time of their release from Bosque Redondo at Fort Sumner some of the Navajo had begun to use the wagons of the white man. It was easier for them to transport both trade goods and their families across the lonely trails of the reservation. They could carry farm implements and haul timber from the forested mountains for their hogans. With the introduction of motor vehicles the wagons began to lose favour and now with the advantages of eight-cylinder pick-ups and four-wheel drive the old horse-drawn buckboard is rarely seen.

With a lightening sky in the north and the moist earth

already sucking in the drying air, the truck pulled out and away from the blotched shadows of the trees. We left the old woman and her loom with its growing rectangle. I thought of its silent birth and remembered for a long time the rug's saturation of colour.

It had been an introduction to members of Mrs Evans's family. She had observed me closely during our visits to the three cabins and my manners had been assessed. An Anglo suddenly arriving at the moment of a threatening storm might have easily caused a reaction far from hospitable. Realizing again that I had received an unusual privilege as an outsider, I thanked Mrs Evans as warmly as Navajo reserve and propriety would allow. A normally undemonstrative person, I often saw the mildest response of enthusiasm on my part as over-generous in Navajo terms. A growing sensitivity to The People's natural reserve made my own interaction with them more relaxed and in many ways their manners were perhaps more northern European than of the non-Indian society surrounding them. There, extrovert social behaviour was almost overwhelming and the lack of restraint sometimes confusing for a foreigner. Among the Indians verbal and social display was in contrast conservative and much more rigid in the interpretation of personal etiquette.

'See that place over there? We know that guy, well I guess most people do. He's another bootlegger. In and out of jail but he runs a pretty big business. Yeh, he keeps on goin'.'

On the return journey to Ganado I sat once more in the truck cab with Bill and Irene. Pointing out to our left to a clearing some distance back from the road, Bill laughed.

'These fellas, they really know what they're up to. I think sometimes us Navajo are pretty crazy.'

In the clearing, matching the red brown soil was a low wood cabin and a number of rickety outbuildings. Tyres and the remains of several vehicles littered the yard and a solitary horse stood with its back leaning against a fence.

There was no sign of anyone amid the disorder and I wondered whether this was one the periods in which the owner enjoyed internment by the law. Or, was he just resting up, preparing for the next Squaw Dance?

Bootleggers are generally viewed by the Navajo as acceptable symbols of irony and, it would seem, are protected within the society by clan and kinship alliances between drinkers and non-drinkers. Even the blatant profiteering, although strongly condemned, goes unchecked because of the law of demand and supply.

One night I asked Henry Morgan, the Navajo owner of Wood Springs' Store and brother-in-law of Bill Draper, what he thought of the Navajo liquor laws.

'I think that a man should decide for himself about how much he drinks. The law won't really stop drinking – well you can see that. If a guy is really determined to get drunk he does it, and if he can't get it from a bootlegger, well, these people get in their trucks and drive over into New Mexico and bring back cases of booze.'

Bill, Henry Morgan and I stood by the porch. It was nearly dark and I had been tidying things around the hogan when the Morgans arrived for supper with Bill and Irene. While the women prepared the meal I had been introduced to the man who at first I had not recognized as the store-owner at Wood Springs. When I arrived in the area, he had given me final directions to the Draper's place.

'Well, this fella can tell you what goes on,' Bill said quietly, his eyes scanning the yard as usual in search of the mad rooster. 'He was a member of the Tribal Council for a long time. He knows what the problems are.'

Henry Morgan looked out over the darkening sage to the juniper-covered ridge a mile or so to the east. The Indian spoke of the mixed feelings and attitudes among the Navajos and their leaders concerning drinking problems.

'Some of the older and more traditional people, they think the law should stay as it is. I think some others who belong to the Peyote Cult which the Federal Government made legal not long ago, want to make the drinking laws more strongly enforced. Maybe this makes people turn to the Peyote religion more, perhaps it makes them a stronger group. I don't know and it looks like the Tribal Council can't decide about any changes – so they leave it as it is.'

One of the women called out that supper was ready and Bill followed Henry towards the door.

'That's our problem right there,' said Bill. 'We Navajos, we're so damned independent, we can never agree about stuff like that. I don't know, maybe there are too many old folks in the council.'

We said goodnight and I went into the windowless hogan with its smells of earth and pine. Sharp shadows were thrown by the hissing lamp up and across the stove's black chimney flue.

'You know around here you see a lot of new hogans. You noticed them over the hill there?'

It was a brilliant morning. Bill sat by the hogan and pushed a stick over the hard-packed earth at his feet. 'There are a number of reasons these hogans are put up. For one thing families get bigger and, as you know, sons and daughters quite often live alongside or near their parents when they get married – and sometimes the aunts and uncles too. Members of the extended family may build there if everybody agrees it's all right. So one reason is accommodation.

'Another reason,' Bill continued, throwing the stick at a chicken about to help itself to corn from the hogan, 'is that the medicine man won't do any ceremonies or anything like that in a frame house. He will only do these things in a hogan with a dirt floor. That's the reason I built mine, the one you're sleeping in. It is of the old way, the medicine men will not change.

'Thirdly, the tribal forestry organization, you saw that big mill up by the mountains at Navajo, they do a lot of thinning out. You know, to let the trees get bigger. The people can get an allowance of about two hundred poles if they do the hauling. There's a lot of poles stacked up around the homes back here.' Bill grinned and levelled the earth with his boot. 'Yessir, we're putting up a lot of new hogans these days. You take that one over there at the Mason's place. They've got one started and we help out some weekends.'

Half a mile from the road running along the valley bottom, to the east along the opposite ridge was the hogan of a Navajo with the unexpected name of James Mason. Apart from some expected Spanish influences in Navajo names a considerable number of families had oddly English names, Draper, Morgan, Hubbard, a Welsh inheritance – Evans and Mason being only a few examples.

Garnet Draper had explained how her husband's Anglo name had originated when Henry Draper's father had first been taken to a mission school.

'That schoolmaster, he couldn't say his proper Navajo name so he says I'll give you my name, it's easier that way. I think that's what happened to lots of Navajos about that time.'

But even with this explanation and the obvious logic I was constantly surprised by Navajos with names from my own country. Interestingly I did not come across any of the Scandinavian or mid-European names so common in older white American families in the American west. These early contacts had been with whites in trading and administrational positions who had, evidently, a strong Anglo-Saxon bias.

James Mason's hogan sat on a rocky promontory overlooking a broad trough of land where corn is grown and horses graze in small fields between bare-sided bluffs. In a few weeks a Navajo wedding with all the traditional ceremonies and feasting would take place there. James Mason's daughter was to be married and Bill Draper was to perform the rites of marriage.

Without a bevy of sons, the Masons were finding it difficult to cope with all the necessary preparations. A new hogan was being built for the young couple and an enormous 'shade' had to be finished in time to provide shelter for the wedding party guests.

That weekend, my last before leaving the reservation for California, I joined the Drapers in their neighbourly tasks towards the wedding preparations. On Saturday morning we drove over to the Masons' hogan. Five of us perched on the truck sides, Porky, seven years old and the youngest of the Draper children, his two older brothers, Chet and Wayne who were sixteen and eighteen respectively, Nathan and myself. Bill and Irene rode up front in the cab and we took the trail down to the road and then south a little way before turning east along a twisting track through the piñon.

Forty yards from the Masons' neatly notched and caulked log-walled hogan stood a newer and larger hogan under construction. With eight sides it was ambitious in size and the log walls were almost completed. A lattice of freshly peeled yellow-white pine logs lay shiny and moist in the sun.

A tall muscular old man worked solemnly at peeling another batch of logs. He wore a chocolate brown hat with a high unpinched crown and a broad flat brim, and he chipped deftly along each log with a large double-bladed axe. Slowly, methodically the dry crusty bark was removed to leave the naked timber lying among the piles of shavings.

Hogan building was his special skill and he had been hired to construct the young couple's wedding present with any additional help carried out under his watchful and experienced eye. I put him in his mid-seventies. He carried himself well, stooping very little with his years and like a number of other Navajos of his generation presented almost a caricature of noble Indian bearing. Now he no longer needed to deal with the problems of ambition or paternal providence, he found his talents and industry still much in demand. Stopping only occasionally to spit and wipe the inner band of his hat the old man worked on steadily and precisely.

Chet, Wayne and I set to with axes on another stack of unpeeled logs trying in vain to keep up with the old man's relentless pace. Inside the Masons' hogan the women talked and prepared food while their husbands finally coaxed a chainsaw into life. Taking turns, they cut the ends from each log already placed in the new hogan's walls, cutting the spare wood back to about a foot from the notched joints at the apex of each of the eight sides. Trimming the horizontally-laid logs in this manner left a neat V-shaped fin protruding outwards from the notched corners and running vertically from ground to roof line. Gaps of an inch or more between the logs would be later filled or 'chinked' with wire mesh and then cement. Hogans of the past were chinked with adobe, a mixture of mud and a binding material such as straw or twigs, and this method was still used by less prosperous Navajos.

When sufficient logs had been peeled for the completion of the walls' full height the old man began at the corners to notch the uppermost logs. Standing on a wooden box he chopped the resting place for the next log with three or four quick strokes of the axe.

As the notching progressed in an anti-clockwise direction around the walls of the hogan the older boys and I lifted up the poles to their new position. After cutting the notches, the old man then hammered a six-inch nail into each one, driving the nail through to the log below for extra strength.

While we worked the younger children scattered through the brush in play. In the heat their voices were muffled and distant. Looking to the south down into the shallow valley I could see a small group of hogans surrounded by fences and split-pole corrals. On the land sloping up from hogans to the west, goats moved among the sparse shadows of stunted pine.

Horses stood dozing with their ears relaxed, their tails making instinctive gestures towards the flies. Figures moved away from the hogans and I watched three long-skirted women lift boxes into the back of a pick-up and then climb aboard themselves as the truck engine started and took them away up the narrow trail to the crest of the ridge where they disappeared.

I was suddenly aware of the quiet. Lunch had been called and the children had rushed to the hogan and the rest of us followed.

James pushed some Navajo frybread across the table. 'Now you'll eat real Navajo frybread eh?'

Mrs Mason, Irene, and – a recent arrival, her mother Mrs Shandi, continued to make the frybread. Patting the maize flour dough in circular motions between their hands the women produced an abundance of the thick Indian pancakes which after being cooked in an iron pan were quickly eaten.

'Those people, down there, where you were looking – they don't like us being here. They give us a lot of trouble while we were building this hogan. This one we're sitting in now.'

Adults sat around the table while the five boys filled the couch and big bed against the back wall of the hogan. Everything was ordered and spotless and the hogan bore the stamp of James's thoroughness and enjoyment of working with his hands. This was a hogan which showed traditional Navajo ingenuity, wedded to the unashamed use of contemporary fittings and attitudes towards décor. A major concession to

Building James Mason's new hogan

convenience and insulation was the joisted and boarded floor which had been planed and varnished. Peeled log walls had also been varnished as well as the main roof support beams. Between each of these beams, insulation board painted white fitted snugly in the triangular spaces and by contrast with the natural wooden beams presented a forceful pattern of spokes radiating from the centre of the ceiling to the log walls.

'Yeh, while we were building this hogan,' James carried on talking through the general chatter now filling the room, 'those people used to drive through here and take down stuff. They did this while I'm working over in Albuquerque. I'd come back at the weekend and find a lot of stuff gone or thrown around.

'Well, you know we couldn't prove anything. Some people – they are like that.'

I imagined that there was probably more to it than that as a number of individuals in the area were considered to be witches. Sings were held regularly for people considered to have been affected by spells and curses, and suspicion among local outfits sometimes led to accusations of witch-craft.

Not wishing to create any difficulties with questions about hostilities between the two groups I immersed myself in eating. Laughing, talking and enjoying the meal the Masons and Drapers relaxed and entertained. Sometimes the conversation would drift entirely into Navajo and then with great politeness Bill or James would sense my disadvantage and explain in English the cause of a sudden outburst of mirth or a moment of seriousness.

Busy with his food, the old man spoke only Navajo, as did Mrs Shandi, at least in my presence, but both were good-humoured and joined the others in making sure that the strangers were shown friendship and hospitality.

Irene's mother was an elegant woman in appearance who like the old man reflected the natural and ancient quality of the Indian. Her hair pulled back in the traditional knot held tightly with white wool framed the broad, well-proportioned face. Wide cheekbones and good skin texture disguised her age and she stood very straight and above average in height.

A large circular turquoise and silver brooch was pinned at the neck of her purple velveteen blouse and her long velveteen brown skirt spread about her fully on her chair by the hogan wall. In her ears were plain silver pendant drops which, compared to the heavy silver and turquoise bracelets, were delicate and restrained. Set against the rich copper tones of her skin the effects of both jewellery and velveteen were undoubtedly regal.

This gathering was interesting from many aspects but not least was the behaviour between son-in-law and mother-in-law. In Navajo society relations between these two are very restricted. A man does not as a rule have any close contact with his wife's mother and meetings are consciously avoided. Even to look at one another is considered taboo and I noticed that during the meal Bill's mother-in-law, Mrs Shandi, had kept

Mrs Shandi, Irene Draper's mother, weaving at Ganado

well to one side and Bill had appeared to ignore her. In retrospect it occurred to me that whenever I had mentioned Irene's mother in previous conversations with Bill he had either tried to re-direct the subject matter or deal with it perfunctorily.

'Mutton and potatoes, yes, and frybread, that's what we Navajos enjoy most. That's our national dish. I hear you guys over in England eat quite a bit of mutton too!'

James was enjoying his hogan being full of people and here, the first Anglo to have received such a privilege fought his way through a mound of sheep meat, swallowing carefully, not daring to reveal that I was not over-fond of the Navajos' favourite food. Strong black coffee was drunk in great quantities with everyone making excursions to the sugar bowl.

'He likes to sing,' said Mrs Mason, nodding towards the old man. 'He goes to all the Squaw Dances and shows those young ones a thing or two.'

Everybody laughed loudly at this and then this was translated into Navajo for the old man. He smiled down at his plate and said something quickly in Navajo at which the others roared in good-humoured derision.

Remarks had been made about the bootlegging activities of Irene's father at a Squaw Dance on the previous Saturday. For reasons the others suspected were not entirely innocent, the old man claimed the bootlegger had not been selling liquor there and had been a perfect gentleman that evening, as he had.

There were hoots of disbelief but the old man remained soberly adamant and the subject was politely dropped.

'We're going up to Fluted Rock to get the oak brush for the shade so we had better leave soon,' James did up his loosened belt and stood up. 'I'll bring the trailer with my truck,' he said, addressing Bill.

'O.K., we'll call back home on the way and pick up an axe or two and meet you there,' replied Bill.

'Fluted Rock is about six or seven miles over there,' James nodded his head to the north-east. 'The tribe does a lot of logging up there and we can take out the oak saplings for nothing.'

Mrs Shandi drove home in her own truck while Bill, Irene, Nathan, Porky and I went back to the opposite ridge to collect axes and a rope. Three miles along the road towards Fluted

Irene Draper's great-grandmother, who wove one of the largest rugs on the Reservation, and was fêted at the Waldorf Astoria, New York

Rock a tyre burst but we managed to reach Wood Springs Store a little further on and change the tyre.

Sitting in the middle of nowhere the store was an odd place serving gasoline and general groceries. It was twenty-five miles to the next place at Chinle. About a hundred yards back from the road its low buildings, sheds, poles and corrals were edged by the ever-present piñon and juniper. Henry Morgan and his wife saw to it that we had the tools we needed and the change was made quickly.

Six miles later we found the Masons. The old man and the older Draper boys were spread out in the forest, hacking down the springy oak. We joined them and worked for an hour to load the trailer and two trucks.

Cutting away in his usual dogged manner the old hogan-maker broke into song now and again, the chanting rhythms of the Squaw Dance.

'Yes, he's ready to go again. That old boy really likes to sing at those dances,' Bill talked as we cinched up the holding wire across the trailer load. 'That fella he won't miss one of those do's if he can help it.'

At the Mason's hogan everyone helped unload the oak brush for the shade. Up on the roof framework of poles, Bill balanced precariously while the rest of us threw up the saplings for him to spread in an even layer. Unloading and arranging the roof took sometime and it was dusk before we had finished. Looking in the half-light at the shade its size seemed even more impressive. Perhaps thirty feet long by twelve to fourteen feet wide and eight feet high it had become a beautifully decorative structure with the close laid branches bristling with their unstripped leaves. It was disappointing to be not able to join in the celebrations but at least I felt satisfaction in having helped in a small way to ensure the Navajo wedding was successful.

As night fell we left the Masons and crossed the valley. Three hundred yards from the Draper's turnoff was a small group of Navajos standing on the opposite side of the road. Four saddled horses grazed close by.

'They're getting ready for tonight,' Irene shouted above the noise of the truck as we followed the rutted trail. 'It's one of the stopping places for a Squaw Dance. Some people up there past Wood Springs are having it. The people will sing there tonight and go on up to the hogans tomorrow.'

This, I thought immediately, is my chance at least to hear the singing and if I was careful perhaps even record some of the songs. Keeping my thoughts to myself Nathan and I returned to our hogan and ate our unambitious evening meal. After this I cleared up, made things ready for the night and put Nathan to bed.

Outside it was a clear night. Stars danced in vast ranks across the cobalt sky. Down across the valley, at the base of the opposite ridge, fires were blazing in the darkness and indistinctly came the sounds of the Enemy Way songs. Collecting my small portable tape-recorder I ducked under the wire of the yard fence and started out across the pasture towards the fires.

Above me the sky retained its purity but at ground level visibility was very poor and my route through the sage and dry grass was more instinctive than selective. Headlights from vehicles turning into the Squaw Dance area on the other side of the valley road swept across the sage in long searching beams. Being caught by the lights was the last thing I wanted and reaching the bottom of the slope I felt a growing sense of excitement and apprehension. It was pitch dark but I gained little security from that with the coming and going of the trucks and was constantly having to fall flat on my face to avoid exposure in the headlights. Like a mindless moth I flapped blindly through the sage towards the fires.

Rising and falling the singing strengthened in volume, the rhythms and chants led by the hataali and his assistants, each song at its conclusion being replaced by the immediate beginning of another without pause. Voices were sharp, sometimes reaching high-pitched shouts. Hair at the back of my head rose and I felt my scalp contract tightly.

Realizing what I was witnessing and aware of the unusual manner of my presence, I did not want to test the hospitality of a large group of Navajos involved in ceremony by appearing suddenly from the darkness, especially taking into account that many were by now well-fortified with alcohol.

Girls shrieked every so often from the darker limits of the gathering and I concluded that perhaps not everybody was involved with the singing and dancing; the night offered additional opportunities. Events, indeed the whole atmosphere of the Squaw Dance seemed to be reaching a feverish pitch. Now lying upon my stomach I tried to blend with the hummocks of sage, and pushed as far as possible from my mind imaginative confrontations with rattlesnakes and scorpions. It was warm but I had to admit the perspiration dripping into my eyes was not entirely due to the night temperature.

If I was to pick up anything at all on the recorder I would have to get closer. Ahead of me about fifty yards away was the road. It was raised about six feet above the edge of the grazing land. Waiting until there was an interval between the headlights, I jumped up and dashed forward to reach the deeper shadows at the base of the shoulder. Running at full tilt I was hit across the chest by something which with tremendous force catapulted me backwards on to the ground. In the shock of impact my thumb involuntarily pressed the recorder's eject button and the tape flew off into space.

Twenty feet out from the road, running parallel to it was a wire fence. In my single-minded attempt to get nearer the Squaw Dance I had forgotten the fence and lay in a state of near panic spreadeagled upon my back. Convinced that every single Navajo had heard me blundering around with wires twanging and the coarse crackle of snapping sagebrush, I lay momentarily paralysed.

Nothing happened and after a minute or two I wriggled back to the fence and, groping around in the dark, managed to find the cassette. It had partially unwound and I had just now crept and crawled across a mile of sage to use the damn thing.

Flames were bursting up higher now and showers of sparks blew across the clearing. Voices were calling out, laughing, yelling, even occasionally screaming and over this the continuous chanting pulsed into the dark. Words were sounds but through that night and into tomorrow would pass songs like the Navajo 'Song of the Earth':

NAESTSAN BIYIN   SONG OF THE EARTH
(Hozhonji-Song)

Daltso hozhoni,   All is beautiful,

Daltso hozho'ka',	All is beautiful,
Daltso hozhoni.	All is beautiful, indeed.
Naestsan-iye,	Now the Mother Earth
Yatilyilch-iye,	And the Father Sky,
Pilch ka' altsin sella	Meeting, joining one another,
Ho-ushte-hiye.	Helpmates ever, they.
Daltso hozhoni,	All is beautiful,
Daltso hozho'ka',	All is beautiful,
Daltso hozhoni.	All is beautiful, indeed

Drawn out in contest the singers vied with each other, performing their ancient chants according to their intensely religious belief in nature and the sacred ways of The People.

No, I would not accept defeat and panting heavily, I began my run, drop, crawl, run across the valley. Once beyond the range of the truck headlights I paused to get my breath. What an incredibly crazy comic situation it all was and I laughed at my own antics.

At the hogan I rewound the tape, put it back in the recorder and set off down into the valley with its distant fires and chants taunting me. Approaching the Squaw Dance again was just as difficult but at least I now knew what to expect. Lying near the fence I held up the tape recorder. My hand holding the small black box rose like Excalibur from the lake and in that position, enjoying the itching but aromatic bed of crushed sage, I recorded for about half an hour.

At last I had completed my task and retraced my steps to the hogan, managing on the way to wake all the Indian dogs across the mesa. Exhausted, I fell into my sleeping-bag and on my back lay staring up through the chimney hole. Faintly from the far side of the valley came the voices of the Enemy Way Chant.

Switching on the recorder I listened to my evening's work. Turned to full volume the playback of the tape produced an almost inaudible muffled dirge of sound in which the clues to the real nature of its source were sparse. As a record it was worthless. For a minute or two disappointment outweighed all my other feelings but then, hearing the singing again through the hogan walls I saw the irony and humour of it all. Now,

almost glad at the technical failure, I reflected on the significance of the evening's emotional experience. Turning my face
into the earth-smelling pillow, I slept.

The day following the Squaw Dance we started to pack the
Volkswagen truck with our boxes and equipment. Nathan was
trying to talk me into taking with us a complete log of petrified
wood. Sections of these pre-historic trees lay in the earth
around the back of the hogan. Fossils patterned with red, pink
and brown rings, a reminder of the ancient tropical forests of
the south-west, their stone trunks now measuring the great arid
deserts of the Navajo lands.

Bill had just returned home and came over to the hogan and
stood with Irene while I told them of the Squaw Dance.

'Hey, you should have said you wanted to go down there.
One of the boys could have driven you down in the truck. You
could have been right there!

'About two years ago we had a Squaw Dance right here,' Bill
spoke slowly and with serious deliberation, as though he was
unsure whether he should say anything about the ceremony. I
said nothing and waited, hoping that he would go on and
explain.

Bill looked into the darkening cloud. 'It was considered,' he
said, 'that I was being affected by some bad spirit. It was my
mother-in-law who initiated the whole thing. The proper name
for the ceremony is the Enemy Way.

'My mother-in-law lives over there in that hogan during the
summer,' Bill pointed up through the scrubby juniper and
piñon on the south-west side of the house. 'It was her that got
the medicine man and set the whole thing up.'

Irene shouted at Porky who, like the others, seemed to
suspect the rooster was a tangible figure of evil and was hurling
logs in its general direction. She turned back, 'Tell him why we
had the Squaw Dance, how we had it and where.'

Bill looked straight-faced at his wife, 'Did we ever discuss the
details in your presence?'

'No, you didn't,' she said, half-smiling. 'I know it's not
allowed at the time but it doesn't matter now – you can say
those things now.'

'Well,' Bill started, 'a lot of families, when they have a Squaw
Dance, they all chip in to pay the man who receives the prayer

stick, the k'eet'oh. Everybody, the family and relatives all pay
something.'

'I didn't want to burden the family so I paid the costs myself.
I paid one hundred and eighty-two dollars in cash and seven
sheep. The other people, they helped with the food and stuff like
that.

'First of all it has to be decided which person is going to
receive the prayer stick. This person must have had an Enemy
Way ceremony at some time for the same kind of "enemy" or
problems. Maybe similar ailments.'

Running off into the trees the boys had left us in quiet. 'Crazy
rooster' had retreated to plan another ambush.

'All the preliminary discussions took place at the Morgans'
down at Wood Springs. We had a hogan built and a big shade.
The person selected to bargain with the receiver of the prayer
stick must decide who to contact and in which direction he
should live. Well, this is discussed by all the relatives first.
When this man has been approached he must give some
indication he wants to receive the stick.

'There must not have been a death recently in his family and
his land and hogan must be located in such a way that he can
put up the dance. It must not be next to a major road or things
like that.'

It was darker still as the clouds moved north and although I
was becoming increasingly excited at the description of Bill's
own Enemy Way ceremony I felt it would be improper to show
it.

'So on the first day the selected person, the sort of spokesman,
visits the individual who will receive the stick and an agreement
is made on the price he is to be paid. Then they break a string to
determine how long this stick is going to be and that it will be
given to him in three days.

'This man says what symbols go on the stick. He says what
should be on the front and the back. The stick has to be made of
cedar and straight – and peeled down to a certain length. The
top part is left and certain stuff is fixed. A bundle goes at the
base and the symbols are carved into the stick.

'Then they work out how long it will take the horses to arrive
at that place. You see, I had to carry that prayer stick on
horseback. Well, anyway, the agreement is made with a man

over there.' Bill indicated to the south past Ganado Lake and over the high ridge.

'That man, he has another medicine man with him in the hogan to make sure that the stick is brought to him properly and that he receives it in the right way. He must be of a different clan to me.

'So to start, we are all down at Wood Springs and I sat in the centre of the hogan while the medicine man who is responsible for things at this end is singing special songs. The prayer stick was already made up and was in a basket. At this point, my relatives bring in bundles of coloured yarn and outside lots of men and boys are riding their horses round the hogan and shooting their rifles in the air.

'My horse is outside and I mount up with the others and they take me over into the canyon down there where a medicine man is singing. He puts two red stripes of paint across my cheeks, just below the eyes. I wear a special blanket and the hataali gives me the prayer stick with the special skins and hair and wood. Then with the stick I get back on to my horse and ride as fast as I can out of there. Out through the canyon, out through the trees and down through all that grazing land until I reached the road up there at Ganado, maybe about four or five miles away.

'In the old days this riding away would be like going into battle – to fight the enemy.

'Something must have happened to me, something pretty strange. They told me later that I came up over that hill and through the trees so fast they wondered what it was. But the funny thing is, I don't remember anything of what happened at the beginning.

'All these riders were around me across the valley – the horses were really going. My horse got too excited and was jumping sideways and after we came out over there, Francis, my brother, he had to carry the stick for me for a while.'

Irene had gone inside the house and Bill seemed to be more relaxed about telling the details of the Enemy Way. Unless it was pure imagination on my part I sensed that Irene recognized Bill's uncomfortable feeling at the boundaries of taboo and had slipped discreetly away.

'When we got to the road, then we loaded the horses into the trucks and drove to within a couple of miles of the place where I had to deliver the stick. Then we unloaded the horses and I ride like crazy to the man's hogan.

'You know it's very strange, that's the only time that horse of mine ever pulled up dead with his legs locked out straight. He usually just gets hold of the bit and stops pretty badly.

'I was excited I guess, pretty high – and I got off my horse and threw the reins to Francis. Then all the horses were fed and watered and looked after. After that I went into the hogan and the people followed me. The man who will receive the stick is sitting with the hataali and he circles my head with his hand and indicates that I should bring it to his feet – and sit down.

'Then he picks up the prayer stick with the carved symbols towards him and puts it in a basket to examine it closely. It mustn't be damaged or have been wrongly put together. If the prayer stick had been wrong he would have passed it back to me and I would have had to go away and come back when it was all right.

'After that the medicine man starts the songs and chants in the hogan. This is to do with how the enemies came and these songs are sacred ceremonial songs, not social ones like they sing later on. Eventually food is brought into the hogan and we relax eating boiled mutton ribs and stew.

'Meanwhile about fifty yards from the hogan all my relatives are fed and looked after. All the visitors are cared for by the receiver of the stick's people. Then the camp is made and the evening starts with a drum being made. The shell of the drum is pottery and it has a skin stretched over the top. I think my mother-in-law still has my drum.

'When that's done the drummer starts the social songs as soon as the sun goes down and everybody joins in the singing. A girl relative of the man who received the stick is selected to carry the prayer stick around all night at the dance. She is the person of honour. I was cautioned by the medicine man not to dance with her, but others could. The men have to pay ten cents to dance with her or any other girl.

'The people start to dance in a circle, sort of skipping and this goes on all through the night with good natured competitions in singing. Groups of the stick man's people sang against my relatives but it was all in good fun and humorous, and very lively.

'I think I fell asleep somewhere in all that. I was pretty exhausted.

'At dawn we all get fed again and then we leave the camp and walk towards the hogan. We made four stops, all the time singing criticisms of the prayer stick receiver. The last stop is outside the hogan where we stand singing in a certain order.

'While this is going on the other people in the hogan throw out gifts through the chimney hole. After four bundles of gifts are thrown out then the people in the hogan they come out and check on the gifts.'

A cat squealed, trapped against the house wall by the two puppies. 'Get that cat out of there, Porky. Those dogs will kill it pretty soon.'

Behind the hogan the sun had pulled its last thin orange streak below the trees and it was nearly dark. Thunder rumbled in the south.

'You know when this soil gets wet you've got a job to get anywhere,' Bill was watching the worsening clouds.

'Anyway, about those gifts. Someone on my team, my relatives, someone had to do the same thing at the end of the Squaw Dance for those people, the relatives of the man receiving the stick.

'That day all the people, both groups, make their way back towards Wood Springs. The stick is carried to within a mile or so of the Morgan's hogan and a camp is set up at that place. When it is night the people sing and dance all through the night again and everybody is fed by my people.

'At dawn the whole party moves down to Wood Springs, well, me and the others on horses race there and then we raced around the hogan and shade in a figure of eight with the rifles being fired in the air. We ride this figure of eight four times.

'After this we dismounted and went into the hogan. By that I mean a group of my relatives. Inside the people sing songs and they all have individual sticks made of tamarix wood shaped like the head and beak of a crow. My little crow stick was tied to my hair.

'Because no women are allowed into this part of the ceremony, unless they are patients, a young boy is chosen to represent my wife. The medicine man mixes herbs with charcoal and then grinds all this into powder and my wife and I are stripped and covered with mutton fat and this stuff. The women do this with my wife separately out in the shade and during all this the singing is going on.

'I'm still in the hogan stripped and blackened with the charcoal and herbs with all my jewellery piled up around me, all the silver and turquoise. This is to do with ensuring my prosperity.

'The medicine man takes me and puts paint, red paint called Cheii, across my cheeks and across my forehead and chin. Pollen or herbs are put on my right side twice – on the woman they put it on the left side once only and she is given a tamarix crow symbol too.

'There was a ceremony for the jewellery then with a strip of buckskin to which certain things are tied, prayers are said over this to accumulate wealth. When this is done they begin singing about the enemy or whatever caused the illness and finally the enemy is named in the middle of the chant and is told that it has been overcome.

'Pollen is put in my moccasin and a loincloth put on me – this was two yards of commercial cloth tied with my silver belt together with all my jewellery. The blackening, by the way, is done by a selected person who gives a gift while doing this.

'The symbol of the enemy is taken out, away from the hogan and this person shoots it with his rifle and offers prayer – then he runs back.

'Over in the shade, blankets are piled up on Irene's back and then she goes to her relatives in the cookshed and gives these to them. Then I go to my relatives and give them presents.

'For the first time since the beginning of the nine-day ceremony I go to my wife's side and we eat blue corn mush followed by other food. Having eaten, gifts are taken over to the receiver of the stick's people – this was a butchered sheep. At four o'clock, or thereabouts, the receiver of the stick and his group have a Round Dance. With this dance there are two circles, the men on the inside and the women dancing on the outside. The group's drummer is joined by our drummer and the people dance until it is dark when the regular dance starts and this goes on non-stop through the night.

'Oh, I nearly forgot, there is a ceremonial chant between the Round Dance and the other social dancing in the evening.

'Next morning everybody goes back to the camp a little way off from Wood Springs and sing until the finish with the Morning Song. During this I undo the skin from my drum and the prayer stick receiver takes the stick and dismantles it and puts it carefully away.

'Well, that's the sort of the finish of it except that you have to stay blackened with that charcoal and mutton fat for four days and carry the crow symbol with you all the time.

'Boy, those are four smelly days!

'You asked me what was my enemy. Well, I was in the Korean War, a lot of us Navajos were.' Bill's face disguised by the darkness showed only faintly the wry look in his eyes. 'A lot of Navajos got wounded too and sort of collected "souvenirs" from the enemy. Yes, hair and things like that.

'I had some health problems and my mother-in-law put the trouble down to this business in the war. So you see the symbol of my enemy was, let's say, some piece of hair and bone. It was this that was taken out and shot during the ceremony. I've been pretty good since then.'

Now the light had gone completely but it had not rained. Like a blue-black sheet, heavy but with an oddly silken sheen, the night sky wrapped the hogan.

Above the trees peered the red earth cones. My last morning of summer on the reservation had come. I slipped under the fence by the wooden sentry-box water-closet and walked out across the cracked earth.

Beneath the junipers the grass had gone, the crusted surface softened only by the silver grey serpentine forms of fallen branches. Smooth-bottomed gullies ran down the slopes, cutting lazily out towards the pasture. There in the strong light and heat three dogs yapped at a herd of grazing horses.

At the lip of the ridge from which the red cones grew, the land fell away steeply. Here a ribbed basin opened out to the lower plateau of Nazlini and then spread north to the valley of Chinle. Beyond that was Many Farms and in the far distance the thrusting buttes before Round Rock.

Wide horns of the ridge curved to the east and west to join stronger ramparts striped in layers of dark rock.

Ochre and black the grasshopper looked at the quartz pebble for several minutes, its little shadow running a blue line over the grey white curve. Flicking at its dark beady eye with a yellow-flecked leg, the insect vaulted across the anthill to a piñon stump where, still and fragile, it savoured a slanting sun.

Part 2

Winter

On the north-facing slopes of the Ganado ridge there were pockets of snow. It was late December as I drove up into the high country once more, feeling tremendously excited but apprehensive.

Would I be able to move back into the family easily? How would the Drapers and their friends react to my return? Now that the novelty of my first visit had passed, the earlier apparent acceptance would be more truly tested.

Dropping down from the ridge I took the road out towards Wood Springs past Ganado Lake. Along the bottom of the valley the road was smooth and empty. Lost from view among the piñon on its east side lay the Masons' hogan. I wondered whether the new hogan for his step-daughter we had helped build had been finished. Had the wedding and all its celebrations been successful?

Further along, on the opposite side of the valley, the cluster of red earth cones fringed with green skirts of juniper and pine came into view. In front, nestled back against the trees overlooking the dripping cold wet pasture was the home of Bill and Irene Draper.

From the road I could see the vehicles were gone, the home empty until the evening. It was now getting on for midday and I thought it more productive to continue on down into Chinle.

Six miles later the paved highway ended abruptly and I began the twenty-five miles of graded dirt road down into the Chinle basin. It warmed a little as I carefully manoeuvred my descent around potholes and hard-packed corrugations of the surface. Two trucks passed going in the opposite direction, towards Ganado, the pulverised earth now powder fine and ploughed into billowing dust trails. Behind the lurching Volkswagen my own dust cloud soon obscured the disappeared vehicles and gradually produced a fine pink film across the inside of the windscreen and dashboard. I could taste the earth of the mesa. In a few miles I had come from moist earth and globs of snow to summer dust.

The old groups of cottonwoods lining water-smeared washes and gullies were gaunt and sad, the flickering leaves of summer stripped, blown away by the winter winds.

A Navajo woman sat at the crest of a small hill across a deep-cut gully to my left. Beyond her I could see west for thirty or forty miles to Salahkai Mesa. Somewhere, out of sight on the other side of the bluff or resting in a hollow would be her hogan. There were no signs of sheep or goats, her solitary vigil unfathomable. I worried about my truck's dust covering her and slowed down but it did little to reduce the thick pink trail. Later an old man in a big hat appeared walking to Kin Li Chee. He glanced only briefly towards me as we passed each other and he carried on, a miniature figure in a great landscape.

Chinle appeared stark and cold without the greenery of the cottonwoods. Compared with the busy and noisy coming and going of people and vehicles during the summer it seemed almost deserted – and strangely still. As I crossed the main road towards the living quarters of the employees of the Bureau of Indian Affairs, Francis Draper walked into view. He was heading towards his home tucked away among the bare limbed trees.

I stopped the truck and called out to him. For a moment he hesitated, not recognizing the Volkswagen.

'Well, hi there. How you doing? You just arrived?'

'Yes.'

Francis shoved his hand through the window and shook mine.

'I drove over from Holbrook this morning.'

'Hey, good to see you again. We got your letter. I think my Mom and Dad got one from you too.'

I suddenly felt things would be all right, the winter with the Navajos would be fine.

'You drive all the way from California again in this funny truck?'

'Yes, this time I came up through Phoenix and the White Mountains. It's hot down there. In California they're swimming in the ocean.'

'Is that right?' Francis laughed. 'Not too many swimming here in Chinle. Oh! Where you going now?'

'Coming to see you.'

'Fine, I'll get in the back.' Francis could see the cab was filled with cases and boxes and jumped up over the tailgate.

At the house we had a lunch of beans and coffee. Ella was out at Del Muerto and so when Francis returned to work I drove up to the national park's centre and informed them that I was again a guest of the Draper family and would be going down into the canyon at some date. Now I had become a recognized friend of the Draper family, I could, as a special privilege, come and go freely into the canyon with all other Navajos.

Water ran in a central shallow stream along the bed of the wash and from Junction Overlook I gazed down into the canyon's hidden world. Silent, windless, the whole view before me seemed eerily still. The stillness held me. It made my ears strain to hear small sounds. Gradually, imperceptibly they came, pricking the silence gently. Below me the rattling monologue of a raven reached upwards from the canyon wall and towards the north at the junction of Canyons del Muerto and de Chelly I saw and heard two Navajo horsemen.

Riding along the packed sand at the edge of the wash the horsemen disappeared towards the west behind the great monolith of Junction Rock, a giant stone loaf growing from the canyon floor. Voices and echoes were lost.

In the intervening years before the first Navajo group moved into the canyon in the middle of the eighteenth century small bands of Hopis used the ancient garden for their own needs. It was probably the Hopi who introduced the peach trees brought into the south-west by the Spanish in the seventeenth century. The fruit was seasonally harvested and taken back to their mesa villages further to the west.

Navajos saw at once the beauty and richness of the canyons and found that corn grew well and their sheep fattened on the grass along the wash. They tended the peach trees with care and felt secure among the natural fortifications of rock. Only rarely did their enemies, the Utes and Apaches, come to the labyrinths of the canyons.

As The People grew in numbers and their reputation as raiders spread across the south-west, the Spanish sent punitive expeditions from New Mexico into Dinetah, the land of the

Francis and Ella Draper with their son Brian at Chinle

Navajo. New Mexico, settled by the Spanish, become a source of plunder for the Navajo. New Mexicans raided the Navajos for slaves and the Navajos raided their frontiers for livestock and Mexican slaves. Horses and sheep became fundamental to Navajo life and as the warriors enjoyed the greater freedom and wider range offered by the horse, so their raiding abilities increased. At this time the Navajos became the most feared of all Indians in the south-west.

Several military expeditions had been made by the Spanish to Canyon de Chelly but had achieved little in the way of dislodging or subjugating the Navajo. In 1846 the United States Government took control from the Spanish of the south-west and in the following seventeen years were spasmodically engaged in a series of encounters and expeditions against the Navajo. The People's raids into the territory of New Mexico had created serious political and economic unrest and finally in January 1864 a military expedition, under Kit Carson, one of the West's most famous men, came to Canyon del Chelly and forced the Navajos, by systematic 'scorched earth' campaigns, to submit to the power of the United States government. With the killing of their sheep, the burning of hogans and destruction of the canyon fields, the resistance of the Navajo crumbled and they gave themselves up to the army. Promised food and clothing, The People, weary and hungry, rode into Fort Defiance and there were they herded together and forced to march three hundred miles to Fort Sumner in New Mexico. The Navajo call this the Long Walk, a journey of humiliation, where only the aged, the sick and babies rode. Two thousand of the nine thousand Dineh held in the four-year confinement at Bosque Redondo Fort Sumner, died of disease, malnutrition and at the hands of the Comanches who found them an easy target grouped together in the treeless wastes around the fort.

The Navajos' release and return to their homelands followed the signing of the treaty of 1868 and from that time The People have continuously tended the fields along the floors of Canyon de Chelly and Canyon del Muerto. In these times of transition and cultural erosion The People still maintain their core of existence, their affinity with the land.

In the spring the tiny orchards of peach trees would come alive again, bringing another cycle of life, its passage absorbed by the ancient canyon's red walls to join the memory of those countless seasons lost in time.

Recent rain had stained the canyon walls darker and harsher than they had been in summer.

The liquid colours of the wash glistened on the swifter ripples, danced into the shadows and then became lost in the transparency of the shallows, an intermittent thin film streaked with silver where slow eddies had frozen.

I was glad to be part of the place again and wandered along the rim enjoying the solitude and late afternoon sun threatened with a bank of heavy night cloud slowly moving from the west.

Winter snows on Spider Rock in Canyon de Chelly (see p. 153)

That evening before supper, a friend of Francis, a man called
Thomas, came to borrow the stock trailer and a horse. We piled
into Thomas's truck, a rifle slung behind the seat, and drove out
to Henry Draper's ranch at Del Muerto. Old Henry and Garnet
Draper were away for the day and as we came up the track the
two dogs ran out barking from the gathering darkness.

The horses, a bunch of four, were black shapes against the
little light that was left. Snorting they circled on the north side
of the old hogan, on the knoll where Nathan and I had camped
in the summer.

We backed up to the long stock trailer parked in the yard and
hitched it to the tow bar. Then, while Francis walked up the

slope to unlatch the gate in the fence, Thomas and I kept to the shadows of the shelter used by Garnet in the summer for cooking.

'We gotta hide from those horses. You have to trick 'em. They won't come – and we can't catch 'em if they see strangers.'

Thomas was laughing quietly.

'Sometimes they will only let little kids near 'em. They know all right when you want to catch 'em!'

Francis had managed to entice the horses through the gate and up to the hogan where the hay was stored. We then closed in and after a few quick dashes through the darkness Francis managed to rope a sturdy mare. With the halter the horse was immediately docile and loaded quietly into the trailer.

Thomas fiddled with the wiring connection for the trailer lights. 'We gotta have some lights. The Navajo police, they're stopping all the stock trailers they see at night – especially those without lights. Lots of rustlin' goin' on nowadays!'

In the northern reaches of the canyon Thomas kept cattle and wanted to get them up before the bad snows came. He had land up around Tsaile just west of the Chuska Mountains and would have to ride up there and bring the cattle back through the canyon to Del Muerto. He had his own horse, a newly-bought registered quarter horse but he needed another for a friend to use in the round-up.

'You come from England eh? I have a niece over in Spain, she's studying languages. She's comin' back here pretty soon when she finishes. Then she's goin' to college here and study Navajo. How about that? It's crazy. She's gonna pay money to learn her own language.'

Both Thomas and Francis roared with laughter.

'Hey!' shouted Francis. 'She's gonna pay good monies to learn Navajo? You have to pay to learn your own language? Nothing makes sense these days.'

On the outskirts of Chinle we unloaded the mare into a high-fenced corral and then Thomas dropped Francis and me off at the house. Ellen, Francis's wife, had returned from helping her mother move into a new home and we sat down to supper with the black unblinking eyes of their nine-month-old son watching every move of the bearded white man.

Francis and I talked long into the night – or rather Francis talked and I listened. He talked once more of the old ways dying with the custodians of Navajo religion, the chanters, the medicine men.

'No, the young kids they don't care really. They go to the Squaw Dances round here but they fool around a lot, drink and fight sometimes.

'You see, they don't understand what the ceremonies really mean. They know nothing. You know, if someone said this or that medicine man had to have a new stick, well these kids they'd just think you picked one up off the ground. They don't know any better. They don't realise that it has to be special wood and then cut in the proper way. There are reasons for all these things. – I see only "old" medicine men now.

'When these old men die not only will the old ways die too but all those things used by the medicine men – those will be gone. Those things which belong to the hataali, his medicines, his bones and prayer sticks, all those old religious things they put with him in the ground. But they're not gonna be any use to anyone six foot under.'

We continued with a subject we had talked of in the summer, the coming of the churches to the Chinle area.

'One time, there was only two churches down here in the Chinle Valley, the Presbyterian and the Catholic ones. At that time they really take good care of the people. Even though most of the people still stay with the old Navajo religions they like what the churches do for them.

'At Christmas time, like now, the Navajo come down to Chinle from all over, from a long long ways off. They come down on horseback and walking – and they have the old wagons too. The women, a lot of them, they. been weaving and bring down their rugs to sell, mostly at the trading post but sometimes the minister at the church – he buys some.

'The Navajos, they give each other presents then, and the churches give presents and everybody brings what food they got, like corn and potatoes – and butcher some sheep. And there's sacks of oranges too and apples and peanuts. Everybody had a good time and feel really good. Some people they only see each other once a year because they're scattered all over the place in the mountains and canyons, everywhere.

'Now, well you have seen all these churches in Chinle? They

just come here to get the Navajo people to join the church. See how many they can get. Each church gets a few.

'We don't all come together no more like those other times.'

Francis tipped back in his rocking-chair looking through the ceiling to his memories.

'It's like my Mom's church, the Presbyterian Church at Del Muerto. People used to travel for miles to get there – many Navajo came together there. Now they split up. Some go to revival meetings. You know, the camp meetings they have all over the reservation.

'Some they go and join the Peyote religion.' Francis smiled wryly, leaning back holding his son against his chest. 'I think I know why they start doing that. Maybe some of these Navajos start wondering about all these other religions and what's happening to them. I think I know some of those reasons.'

Francis changed the subject and expanded his thoughts of young people's attitudes, the price of gasoline, food, what he would do when he returned from the B.I.A. – and his father. The latter was a constant concern of Francis.

Old Henry Draper refused to acknowledge that he was eighty-four and since my departure last summer he had cracked a rib. The accident had happened while he was working down in the canyon but it had been some time before the fracture had been X-rayed and diagnosed. As soon as he could move around the old man had started chopping wood and doing all the normal chores of feeding the animals and marching off to find the goats. Only a few days before my return he had twice walked down the trail into the canyon and back to check the sheds and equipment.

'You know my Dad, he's always been like that. When I was young I used to go down with him into the canyon. When we climbed back up I would be halfway up the trail and I'd see him disappearing over the rim. I was pretty strong then too.

'My Dad, he worked over at the coal mine in Gallup for some time when we was kids and he would be away all week working. Then on Saturday he would walk all the way to Del Muerto, straight across – going up and down, through the canyons, maybe fifty miles. He stayed with us for one night and then he walked back to Gallup to start work.

'Those kids, they don't know how tough the old folks were.

Those people, they had to work so hard all their lives – so now when my Daddy could take it a bit easy he doesn't – he doesn't really know how to.'

Next morning I picked my way around the multitude of holes and tyre ruts to the main road and headed towards Ganado and Window Rock. Cloud banks hung menacingly to the south and west. When I reached the summit it became obvious that the rain falling in the Chinle Valley had become snow at this higher altitude. Among the Ponderosa pines the fall had been heavy. Snow clung to the branches in weighty masses, and the young trees bent over into soft white mounds.

I came down off the Defiance Plateau completing the last of the seventy-five miles from Chinle and entered the modest administrational hut of the Navajo nation, at Window Rock.

At the Educational Department office I quickly found Rebecca Martgan and was graciously received.

Her news was that the education budget was being systematically eroded by the federal government and this might well be a political response to the ambitions of the Navajo tribal government to control its own mineral and energy resources.

In the eastern section of the reservation, north-western New Mexico, are considerable reserves of oil. Some of the larger commercial petroleum companies operate in this area under leases and it may well be that the Navajo do not intend to renew these when the present leases expire. There are rumours of the tribe becoming a member of O.P.E.C. It would be certain that any such moves would be viewed with some alarm by the federal government. If the Navajo took such a position the removal of federal subsidies would be a logical political move.

'There is a huge basin of uranium stretching across a large portion of the reservation,' Rebecca mused. 'Now that must be something the federal government would like to get their hands on. We have coal too, as you know, and that is being moved out at a tremendous speed by operating companies who probably know their lease will not be re-negotiated at its conclusion. Those trucks were passing through Window Rock every few minutes, twenty-four hours a day. I don't think the Navajo realize what's going on. I keep a close eye on these things but I can't do anything.'

Rebecca offered to arrange a meeting with her father out near Klagetoh.

'My Dad will probably leave you to look after the sheep while he goes off for a drink.' Laughing, she continued, 'You'll see how the old style Navajos get along. He's all alone out there. Well, I told you that before in the summer, four months ago.'

Corridors and offices were decorated with paper chains and small Christmas trees. Navajo officialdom seemed determined to celebrate along with the rest of America.

'You're welcome to visit us on Christmas Day. Then you could see how us Navajo have been taken over by all this celebration activity.' Rebecca laughed and I thanked her for the offer and I said I would certainly like to join her and her family.

'The 29th should be fine to take you out to my Dad's place.'

The outer office was beginning to fill with people, including Bill Draper, the other person I had called to see. I felt I had slowed down the wheels of administration for long enough and my conscience insisted I leave.

Bill Draper came into the office and we greeted each other – both pleased to pick up where we had left off in the summer.

'I was just saying,' Rebecca turned to Bill, 'that we could take him out to Klagetoh next Friday, to my Dad's. He wants to visit the folks out there. Is that all right with you?'

'Yes, I think that'll be O.K.' Bill replied.

I left them discussing federal cutbacks, distribution of funds and other very un-Christmassy subjects while I went back to the truck to collect a few presents for Bill and his family. A little later, in Bill's office, just down the corridor from Rebecca Martgan's, Bill and I briefly discussed some of the events which had occurred since I was last with him at Ganado in August.

'How did the wedding turn out? You remember we just finished the shade when I had to return to England.'

Bill grinned, 'Well pretty good really, except that the bridegroom never made it over the mountains until about 4.30 in the afternoon. I don't know, some of the family arrangements got mixed up over there – but anyway we got everything going pretty good, all the food and things like that.'

'Was the hogan finished in time for the wedding?' I asked.

'Well,' Bill shrugged and laughed simultaneously. 'We got the roof on O.K. but the walls never got caulked so we hung white sheets all round the walls and I brought that big rug of mine over and put it on the floor. Yeh, it looked pretty good in the end. I don't think they've finished it yet!

'I got me a good beef cow out of it, you know, for doing the ceremony and all. They said we should take it down to Ganado or some place and butcher it but I said, "Heck, there's a good tree right there, what wrong with that?"'

'So I tied the beef right up against the truck and gave it one hell of a whack on the head with a sledge hammer and that was that. Then we hauled it up to a branch and cut its throat, you know, to let all the blood drain out and then we butchered it out right there.

'The skin comes off pretty easy when the carcass is warm. Anyway we had a pretty good time.'

I left Bill to finish his day at Window Rock and drove down to the store. As I pulled into the parking lot snow began to fall. Sleet at first, it soon turned to large flakes and quickly covered everything. The sky to the west and south, what one could see of it, was like the blue-grey in London. After purchasing my goods as fast as possible I drove out of Window Rock and back towards Ganado.

Although covered now with snow, the road offered reasonable traction and, feeling optimistic, I began the slow ascent to the summit. The snow, pushed by an aggressive south-westerly, began to plaster everything, vertical surfaces as well as road and land. The trunks of trees were soon coated on the windward side and branches drooped quickly under the sudden weight.

At that point, about half-way to the summit, the falling snow was so heavy I could no longer see my tracks in the rearview mirror. Coming now in a blinding curtain the snow began to defeat the windscreen wipers. My vision grew less and less through a gradually shrinking ice-edged triangle. The edge of the road fell away on either side with abrupt slopes. Once off the road I would never get back.

Even with the headlights full on, the oncoming vehicles were increasingly difficult to see. Skid marks crisscrossed the road and the rear ends of vehicles, including my own, were swinging out in uncontrolled menace.

I dared not stop and in the deepening snow, I warily continued on to the summit and along the ridge. All the time I had to peer through the tiny windscreen triangle clear of snow, desperately praying that the occasional truck full of Navajos coming towards me from Ganado would pass me without sliding from its intended line of travel. The Navajos' apparent lack of caution terrified me and I expected to be slammed into the brush at any time.

At last, without incident, I reached the Chinle turnoff and headed north into clearer and warmer weather.

Below the Defiance Plateau the land lay naked – a basin of red earth softened by dry ochre grass. Bordering ridges of purple brown rock were deeply scarred with gullies fringed with yuccas and snakebush. It was peaceful and I began to relax, aware once more of the thin border between success and failure of my life with the Navajo. Even a small mishap, a minor accident to myself or the truck, could cancel the essential freedom of movement among the family. Journeys from one area of the reservation had to be undertaken for a variety of reasons and even a temporary restriction seemed likely to hamper my research seriously. Time was restricted. My health and the reliability of the vehicle had to hold up, at least until I reached California at the end of my winter stay.

With its canyons, formidable strongholds and natural fortresses, this panorama of land before me held the indelible imprint of Navajo history. There had been the retreats and sanctuaries from pursuit, first by enemy tribes and then from Spanish and American soldiers.

On my left to the west lay Salahkai Mesa and behind that the encompassed Hopi lands. To the north were labyrinths of other multi-strata mesas leading to the wild and spectacular buttes of Monument Valley. Behind me, south, was the high plateau country leading to the lands of the White Mountain Apache.

Francis spoke that evening of the Apache, for many years in the past the marauding enemies of the Navajo.

'When I was a boy the Navajo were always telling each other stories about what happened to The People many years ago.

You know we always used to ask our grandmother about those things. When a lot of people got together for ceremonies and things like that the medicine men would take it in turns to tell stories about what us Navajo did in the past. Everybody used to sit quiet, not like now. The kids, they don't sit and listen like you. They all run around, they don't care no more.'

Francis yanked his boots off and stood them by the stove to dry out and then sat slowly rubbing his feet.

'There was this Navajo, he was very well known and we called him Crow Man. He got called that because he always went around with his mouth open all the time. Crow Man told us this story about the Navajo and the Apache.

'One time this Navajo man and his wife are out hunting for food – like rabbits and berries, stuff like that. They find out that a bunch of Apache have come into this Navajo country so pretty soon they are keeping a watch out for these people. The woman, she's pregnant and so the husband he says she must hide in a hole in the ground while he continues hunting on his own.

'So this Navajo goes off and later the Apache come along and see their trail and look around to see what they can find. Later on they find the Navajo woman hiding and they get her and drag her out.

'These Apache, they are pretty worked up and they killed this woman. Then they cut the woman open and take out the baby. When they've done that the Apache go out over there where there used to be big ants' nests, great big ones – some very old Apaches, they cut the baby open and throw the baby face down on the ants' nest. After they done that the Apaches ride off over towards the canyons.

'Sometime later the husband of this woman comes back and finds his wife and baby. He gets really upset and mad – and pretty soon other Navajos hear about the killing and decide they will go after the Apache.

'Well these Apache, they find out that the Navajo are tracking them but they don't care – they think they can easily beat the Navajo. They are so sure about this they don't bother to really run off. But when the Navajo come up to them the husband is so angry he kills one Apache right off with an arrow. So they have a big fight and these Apache they see it isn't goin'' to be easy – so they run off and sort of stop every so often, shooting with the Navajos.

'First of all there may be about twenty-five or thirty Apache but pretty soon they lose a few and the fighting goes on right up through the Chinle Wash and over there towards Ganado. This fighting, it goes on and gradually the Apaches are getting killed one by one and the Navajos keep after them.

'They get a pretty long way and then finally there is only one young Apache left, a boy who has a very fast horse. During the running fight the Apaches change horses all the time, the fast one staying till last when this boy gets him and gets a long way ahead of the Navajo.

'The Navajos want to keep on after this boy but the medicine man, he says, "Let this Apache go. It don't matter we let him go back to the White Mountains and tell his people what happened with the Navajo. When he's done this – he will die."

'So they let him go and the Apache boy gets back to his people and tells them all about what happened – then he sort of collapses, it must have been a heart attack or something like that. Anyway – he dies.

'When the Navajo hear about this they say, "Well, the medicine man he is very good. What he said would happen – it happened."

'This was one time the Navajos got their own back against the Apaches in the old days and all along that way that they was chased lots of places have special names. One place over there is called Apache Hump because that little hill looks the same as the hump on the back of the neck. Some places are called after things that happened in the fighting, like "rock where Apache got two arrows in his leg". Things like that. That's why the route they took is called Apache Trails.'

It was cold, bright and cheerful next morning. Along the rim of Canyon del Muerto overlooking Mummy Cave I inhaled with pleasure the dry sharp air.

A thin covering of ice and snow laced the rims, the shadowed crevices in the ancient rock were packed with the brilliant glare of pure white, the snow-filled spaces marked with the tiny tracks of birds. Prickly pear cactus hugged the ground in pinched winter desiccation, the purple-grey clusters poking through the white skin, still sharp-spined.

Earlier, up at Henry and Garnet Draper's ranch I had been chopping wood and when I finished I thought I would take a look at the north end of the canyon.

Among the stunted trees an occasional small bird scratched among the shreds of fallen juniper bark in search of insects. In the distance a jay called for company and chorusing below in the canyon, a pair of ravens echoed up from a thousand feet of rock-face.

Thin-leaved yuccas sat like squads of green hedgehogs in the snow. Their last season's flower wands, dry and bleached of colour, rising like rods of honour.

Mine were the only footprints wandering the rim. Hogans on the canyon floor were deserted now, silent shells. In shadow, the east wall of the canyon was a cold purple with scabs of thin snow, its rock screes, a reluctant host to a tenacious army of dwarfed trees fighting against gravity and erosion.

The soft splosh of snow sliding from the edge of rounded rocks in the sun gave a gentle sense of things in transition, the natural movement of matter, the passage of time.

Before the Anazazi, the earliest peoples of the canyons had lived in the shallow caves and brush shelters, their passing marked only by fire-pit remains. Now, after the Anazazi – the architects and builders of the old adobe cliff dwellings – the Navajos make their mark with field patterns and peach trees. Once gatherers, hunters and raiders, now pastoral herders and growers of staple diet crops, The People leave the winter cold and ice of the canyon floor for the easier conditions along the rims. When the corn, peaches, alfalfa, squash and beans have been harvested the canyon becomes an even quieter and more mysterious place.

Vehicle access to the canyon, even with four-wheel drive, becomes impossible in the winter months. The wash alternately freezes and floods and only the few steep trails down from the rims allow those who own land in the canyon to visit their holdings. Only tough Navajo ponies and a few mixed herds of sheep and goats range the banks – their neck-bells ringing in cold solitude.

My footprints led me back past the little hopping bird tracks, around the rock slabs and through sunny dips.

On Sunday morning I collected the keys of the cabin from old Henry Draper and started over the ridge towards the rim and the trail down into Canyon del Muerto. My backpack was filled with enough food for two days and hopefully enough warm clothing for the freezing nights. I had long anticipated the experience of a solitary stay in the canyon and now at last the time had come. Eager and excited I strode out quickly through the scattered snow and the light of a brilliant clear sky.

It took some time to reach the head of the trail and by the time I sighted the little cairn of rocks marking its beginning I had warmed considerably. Following the broken and eroded trail that I had first climbed with Francis in the summer I began the descent. At my back the sky to the west was deep blue. In front, the side canyon opened in the deep V, the walls towering above me and far below, the small fields of Henry Draper marked by the clump of cottonwoods were crystal clear in the high altitude air. It was six thousand and seven hundred feet above sea level at the head of the trail, nine hundred feet less at its base.

On the last third of the rock stairway I came level with the ancient Anazazi cliff dwelling. The ledge was on my left, the great overhang shadowing the place where Francis had found the mummified remains of one of its ancient occupants. Sunlight slanted across the rock-face making the scoured overhang a dark crescent above the fragments of walls, their colour blending with the ochre red soil of the cliffs. Dropping sharply away from the trail a ragged gully ran back to the cliff base where it opened out to meet the rubble, sand and splintered rock that make up the slope to the cliff dwelling. How many sunrises, I thought, had moved up from the east rim of the canyon to warm this great theatre of rock? How often had the grateful Anazazi, 'The Ancient Ones', stood up there watching that daily spectacle?

As I came down through the last untidy miles of rocks and out on to the flat canyon floor I was even more aware of the immensity of the sheer walls on either side of me – and of the tranquillity of the space before me. I breathed sharply and respectfully.

Overlooked by the cottonwood grove, the small cabin sat in

squat obstinacy at the foot of a slight rise leading to the small alfalfa fields – now neatly shorn and bordered by wheat-coloured bull grass. The gate in the fence running down the side of the fields had been wired up by old Henry Draper on his last visit and I climbed over the barbed wire and unlocked the cabin door.

In the centre of the floor stood the large cook stove, its thin, steel flue rising straight up through the roof. A rectangle measuring about fifteen by ten feet, the cabin had two small windows, one on the west wall and another looking south across the corn patch. The door, as always in a Navajo home, faced east and opened to the bare earth yard separating the tractor shed and the cabin. Against the south and west walls an ancient metal double bed occupied a third of the floor space and beneath the west window was a small table a couple of feet from the stove. In the north-west corner and along the north wall of the cabin stood odd cupboards and tables piles with a jumble of pots, pans, oil lamps and crockery. Bedding, brooms, buckets and axes filled the two remaining corners, the black cast iron stove the dominant item.

I made the bed, ate a few biscuits, and then walked down to the ice-lipped wash.

Water sounds murmured softly through the canyon while the sun delicately ate the crystalline frozen water along the banks. I waded through the shallow water to the wash, about thirty feet wide at that point, and walked slowly north. Climbing higher, with the warm sun at my back, away from the sandy bank, I could see beyond the diminutive cabin and fields to the box canyon, the trail I had come down now invisible among the rocks and gullies. Above the silver grey cottonwoods, stark and leafless and strangely still, rose the massive red rock canyon wall, an enormous wedge thrusting its time-worn point into this jealously guarded retreat.

I struggled northwards through an ice-bottomed hollow and came again to the edge of the wash where I followed the shallows further into the canyon.

Rising behind a tall band of arching bull grass, its seed ears and stalks hung with small chattering birds, appeared the warm brown earth dome of a hogan.

With each step, quiet, potent images formed and dissolved.

Black first, then grey, then chestnut brown, from a thicket of willow, silent horses moved from the shadows to the damp sand where the frosting of snow slowly melted. The mares unhurriedly sipped the water while a breeze which chilled my ears and hands, ruffled their thick winter coats. In uncanny silence the horses walked in single file to the cottonwoods and disappeared among the skeins of their shadows.

Pausing briefly midstream as I crossed the wash my booted feet were suddenly numb with cold and I splashed quickly on through the pebbles and bleached débris of torn and cracked juniper logs.

Some way on from the hogan I sat down, my back against a rock, and warmed a little while the sun hung at its zenith. At last I was enjoying the privilege of exploring the heart of the canyon, whose very fabric discharged a sense of Navajo history and existence. What white societies tend to define as religion has, by its very nature of needing to be defined, never existed within Indian cultures. The Indians' total relationship with nature and belief in all-pervading effects of supernatural powers forestall any inclination towards a separation of daily life and a natural observance of ritual.

A thunderous explosion ripped through the still canyon. Echoing and rumbling the sound died in the ice shadows and turquoise-draped rims. The sound seemed to come from the next bend in the canyon, behind a knoll of rock and sand jutting from the base of the west wall of the canyon.

Again the air split and vibrated with an explosion. Was someone using dynamite to clear a rock fall? I walked further along the wash and as I skirted a sand bar, I glimpsed a small figure directly on the crest of the knoll about five hundred yards upstream.

The Navajo stood up and fired a high-powered rifle. I squatted immediately, and realized with relief that I had not been the target. Amplified, the report echoed for what seemed minutes. Through my telephoto lens I could see the man quite clearly. He appeared to be merely practising, but as a stranger and an Anglo at that I decided it might not be wise to continue further that way.

At intervals the marksman got up from his prone firing position and, from what I could see, adjusted his sights and reloaded. During one of these manoeuvres I dashed across the wash and energetically followed the horses' hoof prints downstream.

A scarecrow's head appeared above the bull grass growing at the edge of the field. Pushing my way through the six foot high wands, brittle and sun-bleached, I felt oddly secure after the exposure of space and the Navajo rifleman. A narrow corn patch harvested months ago now displayed only stubble among the ridges of frozen earth. Standing in universal pose, the scarecrow stretched out its arms, one pointing north, the other south. A plain full black dress formed the body while blue lemonade cans hung from wooden wrists. Small pieces of red cotton material fluttered from the arms and on the neck pole, the head, a one-gallon plastic bottle, wore a headband in the traditional Navajo style. A long white scarf swung in the breeze. Simple and exact, the scarecrow was unmistakeably Navajo.

Crossing another field I walked downstream for about half a mile and then climbed back onto the trail bordering the wash and continued south.

Narrowing now to perhaps a hundred and fifty yards between them the canyon walls rose up around me – seeming higher than ever. The willows, dogwood and reeds were filled with foraging birds, darting out at my passing in a cloud and then flocking back to their meal as I walked on.

Although muddy in some exposed places, the way south was generally crisp and easy-going, the trail meandering from canyon wall to the bank of the wash with the expansion and contraction of the canyon's width. Along this stretch the width of the canyon varied between about one hundred and fifty to two or three hundred yards. Frequently I was forced to wade through narrow fast-running channels or follow ribbed and sandy bars between wide expanses of thin brittle ice. By mid-afternoon I had fallen into a pattern of looking at and recognizing the variety of mood contained within the canyon's winter face.

My thoughts always came back to the Navajos, the trials of their past and the confusion of their future. The Navajos within the Anglo educational structure seem to begin their learning with optimism but often return to their roots with a mixture of cynicism and, occasionally, despair. Even those who appear to the most sophisticated locals to have assimilated the traits, habits and apparent attitudes of white society occasionally reach a point of desperate melancholy and consciously try to re-establish their relationship with traditional Navajo beliefs. Their inherent need for spiritual strength leads them back to Indian ceremonial life where they seek relief from the pressures and tensions of having to manufacture a life-style which basically provides only opportunities for material security.

As the Indian culture is eroded so the behaviour patterns become erratic. Old values are not questioned, they are simply ignored by many of the younger people. And although the older generation are aware of the disintegration of traditional Navajo social structure they can see no way to stop this.

Before dark I would need to chop more wood for the stove and I began to retrace my steps through the canyon back to the cabin. Already the sun had reached the edge of the west rim, the purple shadows sliding out across the canyon floor.

Back at the cabin I found that the drinking water tank was empty and took an old black kettle down to the wash and filled it with a gritty cold substitute. Drinking water was usually hauled into the canyon by truck but now that access was impossible only the wash and a few springs could supply that need.

I ate a can of tuna fish with crackers, then got a good blaze going in the stove, sorted out the bedding and lit the oil lamp. Outside a sharp frost drew a skin of ice over the canyon floor while stars strung themselves through an indigo sky. Stillness quivered and hushed over the wash.

I knew mine would be the only light in the canyon that night. The Navajo marksman and perhaps a few herders would have climbed up to the rims by now. All the other hogans were locked, empty and dark.

Being alone in the canyon, was an undeniable privilege. Had I been particularly superstitious I might have considered the Anazazi ghosts potentially uncomfortable companions. But on the contrary, I rather enjoyed the idea of being observed by 'The Ancient Ones'. An owl or two broke the silence but there seemed to be little else out in the freezing night air. Cold blue shadows filled the spaces between the cottonwoods as the moon rose eerily above the eastern rim. No longer were the Navajo horses foraging at the grove's shadowed trunks, they were gone across the ice water to pull at the meagre grass down by the willows.

Inside the cabin, once down in my sleeping bag, I could look out through the little window on the south wall and see points of light silently brilliant. A mouse buried itself among the pans and pieces of paper, pausing, pushing, poking and scuttling, moving in the darkness among interesting things. The stove crackled into its last small gesture of energy and then joined the dark in silence, and with me – it slept.

Frozen morning earth made sharp noises under my feet. Iced over almost completely during the night the wash lay as a smooth mottled path. Small birds puffed out into feather balls stiffly eased themselves from a long night. Passing the old ruined hogan near the sand flats I turned south, glancing frequently at the west wall of the canyon where the sun began to bathe the oxide stains and move down towards the colder depths. Underneath the ice sheets the running water accompanied me through shadow pockets and out into the new sunlight. Here the blue grey puddles marked the true channel of the wash, its water impatient to crack the shell and reach the warmth. In the open places the liquid leaked and shone against the frost-etched ice.

Walking became less easy as the earth relaxed its crust and I had to move away from pans of mud to higher stony ground. On my right, back near the vertical walls I occasionally caught sight of a hogan screened behind willows or sheltered by the overhang of large cottonwoods.

At a wider part of the canyon I left the wash and made my way towards a hogan set to one side of a small box canyon. Dotted along the sandy bed of an older dried-up wash course were the green hedgehog yuccas well established in the gravelly soil. As I bent down to photograph one of these groups of plants a wild shout ripped out of the cold air, echoing into an alarming multiplicity of voices.

Immediately I stood up, scanning the darker, eastern canyon wall from which the cry seemed to come.

Somewhere up there the voice echoed again, the words meaningless. I felt much as the Spanish had felt, how the U.S. army expeditions against the Navajos had felt – exposed, impotent.

It was impossible to tell whether I was being rebuked, insulted, warned – or invited to conversation. The violence of the echoing tones seemed to indicate the former – but I could only guess. I felt compelled to move and feigning casual indifference I started towards the wash. From some distance I may have appeared calm but in reality my nerves were electrified by the canyon's amplification of the verbal ambush.

For a moment, a split second, I thought I saw the silhouette of a man a thousand feet above on the rim – but it could have been my imagination.

Echoing back from the rock, rising and falling, one phrase, one shout. Each cry overlapping its predecessor, the words became only sounds bitten into the frost air, stretching out the voice.

Sand hissed under my feet and slid to the ice. I could only remember being there, not arriving, not anything before. Stones moved out of the way and the willow's slender veins were wet in the sun. My throat had the tightness of anticipation, my hands were sheathed in frozen air that pulled at the inside of my skull. The cries had gone, sucked in by the rock. If that had been a threat I no longer felt it. I would know its real identity in time.

It was two or three miles to Standing Cow. Horses were grazing just below a Navajo pictograph of a blue-headed cow twelve feet above the canyon floor. Here, around the horses, were the small fields belonging to Francis's mother-in-law where we had come to cut alfalfa last summer. Now thin yellow stubble covered the ground.

A dog barked and looking back up the canyon I saw a man emerge from a clump of willow.

If this is the caller from the rocks, I thought, I had better stay and see what it's all about.

The horses made a good picture against the base of the canyon wall and I continued watching these as the advancing man dropped momentarily from view. Quite soon the man, an old Navajo, arrived heralded by five dogs, motley in shape and size but uniform in colour – a dull ochre.

'Yaatey,' I called out.

'Ah, Yaatey, Yaatey,' the old man shouted back, smiling.

He came up and he shook hands. In his mid-seventies, I

guessed, the old Navajo was still a tall man. His face showed a natural friendliness, and in his right ear was a small plastic hearing-aid.

Opening his coat he took out the hearing-aid receiver and turned up the volume. I asked the old man his name and he replied in English.

'Ah, my name is William Wilson. Those my horses. They get out through the fence and run off. You just looking around, eh?'

I explained that I was staying in Henry Draper's cabin and that I was a friend of the family.

'Oh yes,' he went on, 'I know Francis, Billy and Tommy and Richard, all those Drapers. My wife is sister of Garnet Draper.'

This was Henry Draper's wife and so William Wilson was yet another member of the extended family.

'Did you call down to me from up there on the canyon wall a little while ago?' I asked and the old man said that he hadn't and looked puzzled.

'I didn't have my rope. This is all I got for a rope to catch these horses.' William fished out a short length of black baler twine.

He laughed at himself and broke into a shuffling run over the alfalfa stubble and chased the three horses out on to the trail. As though at a signal the five dogs went into a frenzy of barking and bolted after the mares. The horses crossed the wash and galloped back up the canyon, the flanking yellow dogs' yelps grown to a mad scream.

After shaking hands again the old man went off across the ice after his clamouring animals.

Alone again I followed the current with its melting and cracking ice for another mile or so and came to the ruins of Antelope House. Sheltered against the vertical canyon wall the structure rose a little above a screen of willow and Russian olive trees not native to the canyon. In a sharp curve the wash swept around in front of the cliff dwelling leaving only a narrow margin of gravelly sand in front of the trees which formed a light barrier before the short shelf up to the adobe walls.

There I photographed groups of human figures and animals painted by Anazazi and Navajo artists. Horses were unknown to the Anazazi so that paintings portraying them can be

Procession of Spanish horsemen – including priests, just west of Standing Cow ruin. Attributed by some to the Navajo artist, Little Sheep

attributed to the later Navajos. At both Standing Cow and Antelope House are some of the paintings of a Navajo called Little Sheep who worked in Canyon del Muerto in the 1800s.

In many places the midday sun had melted the ice and now the wash was noticeably quicker and deeper. It had taken all morning to reach Antelope House and having satisfied my curiosity and photographed interesting details of the paintings I turned back upstream. The sun had reached its highest point above the canyon and for a time it warmed the ground and my back, a brief interlude in which birds and small animals basked as well.

As I passed Standing Cow I looked through the overhanging cottonwood trees to the line of mounted men painted across the cliff face. Horses and riders filed in simple silhouette, the men wearing broad-brimmed hats and carrying what appeared to be rifles or swords. A Spanish expedition passing through the canyon in the nineteenth century seems to be the inspiration of this painting, a succinct record of the spread of foreign concern for the Indian strongholds of the south-west.

I continued along the well-worn trail on the left bank of the wash following the horse and dog tracks of William Wilson's animals until these turned away into a side canyon and I followed my own boot marks.

About five hundred yards south of the scarecrow, lounging against a boulder, I came up to another old man. He lay comfortably in the last of the sun while his saddled horse cropped the dry grass nearby.

'Yaatey,' I called out to him in passing and he offered the same in return. Most likely he had come down into the canyon to check his sheep or horses and was now resting before beginning the climb out. It was very quiet. Only the musical jangle of the horse's bit and the rough rasp of the tearing grass interrupted the peace. The Navajo daydreamed perhaps of the old times. His gaze took in the east cliffs of Canyon del Muerto, the Canyon of the Dead, its ice, its stained rim rock and defiant juniper. As long as the canyon was there, his expression seemed to say, the Navajos would have their belief in the harmony of their lives with the land.

The old man dreamed in the afternoon while I walked on to the cabin and prepared myself for the hike out of the canyon. I packed and left the cabin in good order, then headed west for the mouth of the trail canyon.

It was four o'clock and I had been walking more or less non-stop for six-and-a-half hours and the muscles in my legs were cramped and tired.

I crossed the soft sand floor which would soon freeze again as the shadows lengthened, and paused briefly before beginning the trail ascent. As I looked back at the looming escarpment a rider trotted over the rise now concealing the cabin.

The Navajo was perhaps in his early forties, heavily built with a strong face. His slightly hawk-like nose and high cheekbones caught the redness of the rocks and low sun while a white headband fell past his traditional hair knot to the middle of his back.

I was on higher ground just off the trail and we exchanged the Navajo greeting as he passed. His ease in the saddle, the sharpness of his features and the flowing scarf could have been those of a warrior – not so long ago, when 'Dineh' rode out as raiders against the Mexicans and Pueblo Indians. Then, skirmishes with Utes to the north and the Apaches south, had honed the Navajos into feared fighting men who ranged far and wide across the south-west in search of plunder and slaves.

At a steady trot the man rode on. In the growing dusk, his white horse was almost luminous as it picked its way along the trail and into the first tumble of rocks.

For some inexplicable reason I felt magnetized by the horse and Indian, following them as fast as I was able to walk with the heavy pack. The Navajo stayed mounted as the ascent began and I was certain that I would catch up as the trail became steeper and rougher. As I too began the real upward trail the Navajo disappeared behind the rocks but, with a peculiar urge to catch up, I pushed on at a pace which soon had me gasping for breath.

At an irritating distance the Navajo and his horse came into view. I stopped for a moment to catch my breath and quickly studied the next series of steps through the rocks, glanced up and found that the Indian had gone. I heaved myself over the obstacles of the trail, legs aching with the strain of walking all day, and continued to scramble upwards.

At last fatigue, if not common-sense, halted me. In taunting repetition the Navajo appeared again on a much higher ledge, this time on foot leading the horse by the reins. They were as ghosts in the half-light, looking down as I looked up.

Now and then I caught further glimpses of the two figures moving higher. Finally they stopped at the crest of the canyon where the horse, a mysterious blue white, glowed before the two became small black shapes – then disappeared.

Hoofmarks in the snow and ice gave me an easy trail to follow and, where on my own I might have taken a wrong turn, they at last brought me to the rim. I had come out of Canyon del

Muerto from the place called Twin Trails, and it was Christmas Eve.

'That guy in the canyon with the rifle, I think I know who that was.' Francis shoved the ham and eggs towards me across the breakfast table on Christmas morning. 'Those people are crazy. Probably a good thing you stayed away from that guy. I don't trust some of those people. He was herding sheep I think. They were probably further up the canyon – or round that bend.

'Last year this other guy, he has some bolts loose, he's crazy, he went right down through the canyon breaking into all the hogans. I had two trophy saddles in the shed by the cabin. He took those out and some bridles. I guess he thought he would catch a horse but he didn't make it and just dumped the saddles out there by the cottonwoods.

'Hey, there's more bread here – if you want it. Help yourself.

'Anyway, some other guys found him down at Standing Cow. They tried to get him but he had this big rifle so they left him and got the police. Well, he went to jail for a while but he's back out now. He lives right up there on the rim above Antelope House and he stays up there. People don't bother him too much – he's still got that rifle.'

I had not mentioned my experience of the shouts from the canyon walls near Antelope House. Now suddenly it occurred to me that the rifleman of the day before and the hidden watcher might well have been the same person. Perhaps my feeling of apprehension had been justified.

'Yeh,' Francis blew over his coffee, 'that William Wilson he used to be a real big fella. Sometimes he stays down in the hogan just down from Standing Cow, in that little canyon off to the side. His family live on the rim above there. Yeh, he's all right.'

Through the window I looked at the thin trees, dry and cold, stuck in the hard earth. Like them, the wooden fence was grey and withered, flayed by the winter winds. Along the track past the house a stiff-legged dog sniffed the posts, and the garbage can. He must have been disappointed for he passed by marking the can with a staining splash.

Someone called back among the trees, another dog yelped

and a single gunshot cracked some distance to the north out near the wash.

'All those horses you seen down there in the canyon. See, that's what some Navajo do. They let 'em run around all over the place.

'Like this trouble we have with the Hopi. They got lots of trouble over there. You know the Navajo who live over there by the Hopi, they just let all their sheep and horses run all over and eat up everything. Those Hopi, we had trouble with them a long time but the Navajos don't care. They say it's all right if the sheep and horses go over there.

'Anyway the Hopi got new laws from the federal government and they are putting up a wire fence all the way round the Hopi reservation to keep the Navajo stock out. And all those Navajo inside that fence the government say they will find new land for them to live on. When the agreement was made they [the government] said they had got the land for the Navajo – now they got the fence up there don't seem to be any land anywhere. You can't find land here – even when you see big bits of land which you think is empty Navajo already live there.

'The Navajos over there get mad and cut the fences and pull up the steel posts but the Hopi put 'em back up. When they see the Navajo they say "you go away and leave this, if you come back we shoot you." That's why all the Navajos over there carry guns all the time.'

We finished eating and went back into the living room and sat by the stove.

'This Navajo woman,' Francis prodded at his teeth with a toothpick, 'she went over there and cut the wire and the Hopi got the police and they put her in jail. A lot of Navajos marched from here to Washington about this business. I don't know how long it took them, but nothing happened. The Government spend millions of dollars on that fence. They're not going to take it down now. Those Hopi know it too.

'Well, Merry Christmas oh! I tell you something, this story about this Navajo lady. It's a joke, don't take no notice of this.

'This old lady she has this bad back and she has lots of aches and pains. Her relations say "you should go over to Kayenta and see that Hopi medicine man, he can get rid of that trouble for you". So she says "Well, maybe I will, I don't know."

'With her all the time is her grandson and he likes to look after his grandma. He says, "Sure Grandma, you should go over there, I'll come too and look after you."

'His folks say they don't want him to go, he shouldn't see those things anyway. But the boy he still wants to go with his grandma and says, "It's all right, I have to look after my grandma, she needs me over there."

'So finally they all say, "Well – if you want to go that bad, you better go."

'So the boy and his grandma go over to see the Hopi and he says he can fix the trouble for twenty dollars. The Hopis say that boy he can't come in with his grandma – he's not allowed to see these things. But the boy he goes right ahead saying that he has to be with his grandma – no matter what they do. So in the end the Hopis say, "Well, all right, you can come into the medicine man's house."

'Then they take the old lady's shirt off and she lays down and the Hopi has a look. "I think someone has put a bad curse on you," something like that. "I see there is a little stone thing in your back but I can get that out all right."

'Then the Hopi starts sucking this one spot on the old lady's back while the grandson watches all the time to see what the Hopi does. Pretty soon the Hopi sucks up the skin on the back into a little sort of mountain and he says, "Don't worry grandmother I will soon have this thing out."

'The people standing round, they see the medicine man has nothing in his mouth and then pretty quick he gives one big suck and then spits out this little tiny stone into his hand. He shows it to the Navajo woman. "How do you feel now Grandmother?" the Hopi says.

'The grandmother stands up and straightens her back. "I feel really good again, that was really strong medicine."

'So the boy and his grandma leave the Hopi and come back to their people and she is really well.

'The boy is herding the sheep all summer in the canyon and one day he picks up this shiny little stone from an ant's nest. You know those little stones, like a little garnet. Well, he puts it up his nose and breathes it in through his nose into his mouth. And all summer he practises doing this until he's really good and he knows how that Hopi fixed his grandma.

'One day as the winter was coming on the boy's grandma says she don't feel so good. Her back is bad again. So the boy says, "Don't worry I can fix that. I can make it better just like the Hopi did."

'The boy's parents hear this and tell him not to be stupid. "What do you mean you can fix your grandma's back? Course you can't do that."

'But that boy he keeps right on till they say, "O.K., if you think you can do it you better try."

'So they take off grandma's shirt and the grandson puts the little stone up his nose when nobody is looking. Then he say "Hey Grandma, I know what the trouble is here, there is one more little stone up here near your shoulder."

'Like the Hopi he sucks up the skin till it's really pinched up, then he shows everybody he has nothing in his mouth.

' "Here it is," the boy says and spits out this shiny little stone into his hand. Everybody is really surprised. He says, "How do you feel now, Grandma?" And his grandma gets up and she puts her arms right up over her head and stretches and she says, "Grandson – I feel really good." '

Francis and I laughed our way into Christmas with the sun on the frost right across the Chinle Valley.

At noon I collected Garnet and Henry Draper together with Hank, their grandson, and drove them from the ranch at del Muerto to Bill Draper's home, forty miles away at Ganado.

Hank was very fond of his grandparents and the ranch, and spent most of his school holidays there doing odd jobs and seeing to the animals. The relationships between old and young within the Draper family showed natural emotional ties but also the special Navajo obligation to look after older family members in practical terms and – to recognise the emotional needs of old age.

We had all been invited for Christmas dinner and as I was due at Bill's home anyway it seemed a very suitable occasion to begin my winter tenancy.

Far more frost and snow affected the Ganado area than at Chinle, especially along the ridges toward Kin Li Chee. Red in the summer, the beehive combs of earth and rock behind the hogan were now white above the juniper and piñon.

I picked my way to the house, trying to avoid some of the

ankle-deep ruts but I skidded and bounced from mud to snow to cracking ice. Bringing Bill's father and mother to Ganado made me feel far less apprehensive at my return to the family. Smiling faces filled the room when I entered the home and the relaxed atmosphere with its buzz of talk and humour assured me of my welcome. Without any sign of nervousness or reserve the Navajo family had come to regard my presence as perfectly acceptable, even, it seemed, enjoyable.

Twelve of us sat down to dinner, a traditional American-style Christmas dinner of turkey and cranberry jelly, corn, potatoes, beans, sage stuffing, peas and small cakes of bread. Bill and Irene with their four sons, two daughters and a granddaughter, Henry and Garnet Draper and myself ate to the point of immobility.

In the house was a decorated evergreen tree, in days gone by a symbol of pagan European fertility rites which now focussed attention on the birth of a Jewish Messiah.

At intervals I thought with some amusement of the irony of eleven Navajos and one Englishman celebrating Christmas together with such mixed cultural backgrounds. Under the eaves of the front porch hung bunches of blue corn, a good luck symbol of the Navajo Holy People. The hataali chanted for the spirits of the Navajos but in town was heard – no doubt – Christmas carols!

Presents were exchanged after the meal and even Nathan in his absence had been remembered. I accepted his gift, promising to carry it carefully back with me to England. I had to remember that the Navajos give and receive presents in a very different way from what I was accustomed to. Indeed, Grandma and Grandpa Draper accepted their wrapped Christmas gifts with completely dead-pan expressions and put them to one side, presumably to open them later at home. The children, even the youngest, received presents from their parents and grandparents without displaying any of the normal signs of unbridled enthusiasm expected in Anglo society. Nor did they temper their receiving with any show of gratitude and carried their presents away to corners of the room where they were quietly and privately opened and inspected.

We talked for a while and then, while Bill drove his parents back to del Muerto to check the stock before nightfall, I moved into the hogan and organised my belongings amidst the comforting chaos.

Within the hogan my feelings were of security, relief, and immense pleasure. Its familiarity prompted thoughts of the beginnings of my association with this segment of the family at Ganado. The hogan had become an expression of the relationship between myself and the Navajo family. Before my arrival, I had seen the hogan as a point from which my understanding of the complex problems of Navajo life might naturally grow.

All the ironies of transcultural influences were there in the paraphernalia in the hogan. There were the piles of boxes marked with federal government legends which qualified the use of their contents with instructions forbidding their sale privately: saddles, cupboards, tables covered with bedding, forks, shovels, axes, bicycle wheels, chicken feed, a battered armchair covered in P.V.C., lamps, buckets, boxes of tools and palliasses lying on the earth floor. An earth floor for the hataali.

Instead of the old single cylindrical woodburning stove a cast-iron potbellied newcomer held pride of place beneath the chimney hole – its boldly embossed trade name FATSO obviously appropriate. Reorganizing an area in the hogan I made space for my own food boxes and assortment of cases and equipment and then set up a camp bed. Freshly split juniper logs gave off the keen scent that had now become associated with my life on the mesas and in the canyons of the Navajos. From the chimney flue the white smoke drifted into a white dusk.

Later that evening, as I sat lost in my thoughts beneath the hogan's ceiling patterns and soaking in Fatso's luxuriant heat, a Christmas guest arrived.

'Hallo there, we heard you was here. Didn't really expect to see you out this way again. We brought you something. It's just some little thing.'

At the hogan door I found James Mason and his wife. To one side stood two attractive daughters, both attempting to disguise their obvious curiosity but failing delightfully with spreading smiles.

James presented me with a bulging small brown paper bag. 'We only got one day when me and my wife are off work together. She's changed her days so we can't get out here too often. We're living over at Fort Wingate as you know. We come over when we can to check the hogans. We never finished the new one yet – maybe when you come back in the spring it will be finished.'

The Masons had offered the new hogan to their stepdaughter and her husband at whose wedding Bill had officiated last summer, but the man was unable to find work in the area. Like the Masons and other Navajos without sheep or cattle and caught in the complexities of wage earning, the young couple had to rely on the busy commercial centres such as Albuquerque and Gallup for a steady income.

'When I retire,' James said, 'I'd like to come back to Kin Li Chee and maybe run a small store and keep some sheep.

'You know,' he went on, looking straight at me and laughing, 'we're still looking for a nice squaw for you, a good Navajo girl.'

Both his daughters giggled and looked intently at the snow about their feet.

'I think that would be really good,' he added, his wife joining in with this line of proposition and amusement. 'We see what we can do by Easter time.'

I thanked them again for the present and their general concern for my comfort, forgetting that such obvious gratitude was not expected, and when they had gone sat down by the stove and opened the paper bag. The contents immediately struck a chord from my childhood, when in the excitement of a dark Christmas morning the sock at the end of the bed, misshapen with intriguing lumps, was spilled on to the eiderdown. My present was simply an apple, a mixture of boiled sweets and unshelled peanuts. From anyone it would have been a nice gesture, from a Navajo I had known only a short time, who had come to the hogan door on Christmas night, it was for me, marvellous.

That night it began snowing and by morning the land was completely white, the trees caked with hoar frost and snow, and the valley to the front of the hogan brushed smooth as a sheet. Blades of ice hung from the hogan eaves where the escaping heat from the stove melted the snow through the thin board roof. Snow fell gracefully through the chimney hole to hissing oblivion on the top of Fatso, the descending fine white shower around the black stove pipe creating a peculiar column of dark

The author: a winter's night in the hogan at Ganado

and light. The specks of falling snow mesmerized me.

I was able to do little other than keep warm and organize the hogan, sorting what foodstuffs I had, collecting wood and occasionally looking out at the deepening snow.

Flurries of white continued down through the hole in the roof, spluttering and dissolving on the stove while I read beside it with my feet up on a pile of drying logs. Around me the hissing lantern's low circle of light made soft shadows while the woodstove draught rumbled in search of the black flue. Juniper logs gave scent to the cold outside air.

With the snow had come a creeping veil of fog. To leave the hogan was to step into a world in which earth and sky were one.

Without windows the hogan's only natural light came from the chimney hole and to step from that muted interior into the snow was momentarily blinding. Sorties to the sentry-box were carried out in a tortuous squint-eyed shuffle. The intensity of reflected light I always expected to diminish after a while – or rather that my eyes would adjust. They never did.

For three days it was impossible to reach the road by truck. The entombing fog drifted this way and that and the only way of getting out at all with a vehicle was to travel late at night or very early in the morning before the track's surface softened.

In this period I lived as a hermit within the hogan, keeping the woodstove going and making entries in my journal. At night it became colder than ever, my water supply freezing solid in its bucket – inside the hogan.

I missed going out along the ridge for my daily walks but such exercise was pointless with such poor visibility. To keep my blood circulating I did, once or twice, stumble around among the juniper, following rabbit-tracks for a while – but the freezing fog soon stiffened my beard and eyebrows and I went back to the muttering stove.

White upon white, the land kept its silence. Junipers along the ridge stood cocooned in snow. Each clump of frozen twigs became a massive fist of fog crystals in the rasping night temperatures, and their forms turned the land by daylight into a fantasy of icing-sugar trees.

With the dogs running eagerly ahead we made trails daily across the snow, crossing gullies with the tracks of long-eared bobtails leading me up to the ridge. Along the exposed crest the juniper and piñon were even more heavily encrusted with frozen fog and were devoid of branch or needle. It was a floating space of land and air without division.

Parents and grandparents have experienced great hardships, disillusionment and often betrayal, but within the pattern of their lives has always been the knowledge of The People's history and the spiritual unity of 'Dineh'. This was held as the core of their existence, to be fought for if necessary, and for every Navajo there was personal responsibility. The Navajo's way of life was strengthened, sustained and acted upon daily and, for the Navajos, it was right.

Education forcefully imposed in the early days by the United States government formed the first deliberate manoeuvre intended to break down tribal cohesion and fracture the social and religious codes of The People. As a consequence of these early educational policies, family ties and identity also began to be diluted.

The boarding school system, for practical and economic convenience, still exists across the reservation under federal and state structure, and many religious denominations encourage and finance boarding schools for Navajos off the reservation. Educational opportunities are determined to a large extent by the vast distances within the reservation and the scattered and remote locations of family hogans. All of this, however well-intentioned, must contribute to the problems of the young Navajos' ability to digest the cultural and social diet of another all-encompassing world in which both past and present values are vastly different.

Social welfare programmes initiated and maintained by the Federal Government and the Navajo tribal government extend, by the broadening of choice, the confusion and frustrations of the young Navajo. Even the older generation, to a considerable degree, have become over-reliant upon monetary and commodities aid programmes. Child benefits, housing aid schemes, food supplements, animal husbandry grants, clothing allowances and other policies have eroded the independence of the Navajo.

The lack of land management contributes to the difficulties in both environmental control and agricultural development.

From the attitudes and criticisms offered by many concerned Navajo the tribal government has not given proper attention to the development and marketing of stock. Cattle and sheep are still regarded as symbolic of traditional pastoral life rather than as an important economic ingredient to the Navajo way of life. Population increase threatens to bring an acute shortage of land and with that the thorny problems of future land usage.

Land has always been regarded by the Navajo as something to be enjoyed and used by all, like the air. Unfortunately, as natural and logical as this is in an agrarian and pastoral society, this has led to the drastic effects of overgrazing in a land largely destitute of water.

'You see, it's like this,' Bill spoke, leaning against the hogan wall. 'I only know one man round here who really knows what's happening, at least to the land he's always used. He knows it's been overgrazed.

'He'll say to me, "Look at that over there, it's just sand dunes. What's the good of me letting sections of the land round here lie fallow? If I graze my sheep away in the other direction some other Navajo comes along and lets his sheep on it. He thinks no one is using it. It would take maybe three years to get the grass back. You can't force it, so it will never get rested."

'Once they used to say,' Bill went on, 'the old folks that is, "the grass was always up to a horse's belly and we were never short of water." Well, they forget we were a lot more spread out then and not everybody had sheep and horses. Maybe in some areas the grazing got pretty bad but, now if we're not careful the whole reservation is going to go like that.'

During the day when the stove was alight I could hear the icicles crack and drop to the ground from the eaves of the roof. The thin modern board roof allowed much of the heat to escape, leaving only a narrow collar of snow at its lower edge. Although snow no longer fell the nights were increasingly colder and I was unable to keep the stove burning the whole time. Every morning I found a thicker layer of ice in the water bucket near the cold black Fatso and the ground outside iron hard.

New Year's Eve passed with the sound of four rifle shots fired in quick succession from across the valley. Next morning I awoke to the raucous calls of a pair of crows. The birds flew low over the chimney hole and, in their slow, almost casual flight, turned to look at me. Whatever significance that might have had I did not know but, rather strangely, the performance was repeated that evening when the birds returned from the east.

That day, New Year's Day, I drove seventy miles to Spider Rock Overlook on the rim of Canyon de Chelly. I wanted to see again those two giant fingers of stone thrusting upwards from the canyon floor, this time, for a change, without the sun's vibrating heat.

Thick layers of snow overhung the rock shelves and the sky was only weakly punctured at intervals by an unambitious sun.

At the juncture of a side canyon to the main Canyon de Chelly the two red fingers rose from the edge of the icebound wash. They defied the cling of snow and only upon the very top of the tallest pinnacle was there a thin powdering.

Except upon the eastern walls, as in Canyon del Muerto, only the canyon floor carried the bleaching of frost with the wash a band of steel grey lipped with white ice. Two hogans small and lonely, their log walls almost invisible with the foreshortening of a thousand feet of height, stood on patches of flat scraped earth half a mile apart on either side of the wash. Around them the mighty background of rock dwarfed them.

Spider Rock, a magic and special place for the Navajo, soared upwards from the ground, piercing the space above it. I stood for a long time, feeling its presence, thinking of its silent awesome witness to good and bad, to veneration and subjection. These canyons had known more than water and sunlight. The primitive hunters, the earliest wandering groups searching for food and shelter, must have thought it the very eyrie of the spirits of their world and that beyond. After them had come 'the ancient ones, the enemy ancestors', the Anazazis with their cliff-face villages. In their firelit underground ceremonial chambers, the kivas, the chants and the sounds of the dancers' stamping feet had echoed out. Children had laughed and shouted in easy times, scampering up wooden ladders and along the narrow ledges. Adults had tackled the business of building and masonry, enlarging and adding rooms to their precious communities lodged beneath the massive overhangs of rock. Below the cliff villages were small gardens irrigated as they are now by the waters of the canyon wash.

Then quite suddenly, after six hundred years or more, the Anazazis began to move away into what is now northern New Mexico. Severe drought in the thirteenth century and perhaps the pressures of marauding groups of people from further north may have caused this abandonment of the cliff dwellings and by the beginning of the fourteenth century the canyon was largely empty, the kivas silent, the voices of the singers kept only by the rock.

On the journey back to Ganado I moved down from the dazzling brightness of the rims where a late but victorious sun clipped low wedges of shadow to the foggy Chinle Valley. It was sombre and brooding – with fog cloud drifting low at first. Then, as I drove towards the ridges, it spread and thinned to expose the vast plain edged in the distance by Black Mesa, its flat top, cold, remote, held by a halter of grey white.

A black speck, a single horseman followed an almost invisible line of sheep across the endless white plain.

'When The People were over there at Fort Sumner some of the soldiers, especially those Mexican ones, they got after the Navajo women and did bad things – but nobody could do anything about it.' Francis looked over at me and grinned, he reflected upon one story.

'Quite a big group of Navajos were making their way out from Fort Defiance after they were allowed to leave Fort Sumner in New Mexico. One of these Navajo women was pregnant and the other people knew it was from a soldier. This woman was close to the time of having her baby and a lot of the Navajos said "Why don't you get rid of that baby, we know the father was an enemy. Why should we have more of these people? We don't want the children of our enemies, there are too many already."

'But this woman, she kept right on, sort of keeping out of their way and quiet. Pretty soon she goes off in the trees and has the baby and brings it back to where the people are camped. At first they don't say anything but as they keep moving along towards their old homes the men get angry. And they start telling this woman she has to kill that baby because it's the enemies'. For a while she keeps on going, thinking everything will be all right. But these other people say, "You have to leave that baby." Well, this young woman is crying and everything but she knows she has to do what they say. So she takes the baby and puts it in some bushes and goes back to the people and says she's left the baby. The people then carry on their journey with the woman really sad because she's lost her baby.

'Some way behind this first group of Navajo is another group coming along the same trail. These Navajo they eventually come up to the place where the first ones made their camp and they make their night camp there too. In the morning some of them hear noises like a baby crying and when they look around they found that woman's baby only a short way off from the camp.

'These people they say, "Well we can't leave that baby like that – it wouldn't be right. It's only a little tiny thing." So they pick up the baby and take it with them when they leave.

'Up ahead in the first group of Navajos, those people who made the woman leave the baby, they are beginning to feel bad about everything. They begin to be sad that they made the woman do that. Anyway, later on this second group catch up with the others and when they get to their camp they show them the baby they found on the journey. Well, the woman recognizes the baby as hers and everybody finds out what happened. The woman's people, they say "We did a bad thing, the baby should stay with its mother." Well – the woman is really happy that she has her baby again and that she can keep it. After that everybody is pleased and the Navajos go on to their lands and their hogans.

'That baby that was born on the journey was my great-great-grandmother. That's the reason some of my family still have sort of wavy hair sometimes, like my Dad and Richard and me.'

Cold wind pushed the Navajo pony's tail between its legs and the girl's hair streamed forwards from beneath her head-scarf. Around her shoulders, pulled tightly, was a red and blue blanket, the corners tucked around her thighs flapping impatiently.

She came along the ridge with the north-east wind at her back, the blurred line of sheep strung out behind her. Two dogs, black heavy-coated animals, padded in the tracks of the sheep, their heads low. Clumps of thin-leaved yuccas pierced the snow at the mesa's edge inviting the eye to pause and rest a moment.

The girl with the red and blue blanket grew to a silhouette against the white fog sky as she picked her trail down the steep slope. White-fluffed, the sheep followed the pony's tail with three lambs collared with red ribbon among the leading animals.

The pony was black with a white blaze and it kept its rhythm on the long slope down from the wind-cut mesa to the shelter of the piñon. There were no sounds other than the soft hiss of air shredded by the branches.

Muffled at first but bringing a clearer note as the sheep emerged from the blue-grey trees, the neck-bell of the first sheep announced the herd's approach. The girl, still with eyes only for the way ahead, passed from the dark contrasts of the mesa into the clearing where the two trails converged. Her eyes, dark within a writhing frame of black hair, looked only for a moment in my direction, her expression secret and then turned away to the snow-covered trail.

Slowly the sheep and the figure on horseback returned to the white fog. The red and blue blanket and the black pony dissolved into that white space.

Roasted mutton ribs were served for supper and I had been invited.

'You know, just before you got back this morning, the kids and me had to butcher this sheep in the back of the truck. It was some size,' Irene's face creased in an impish smile and she offered the large plate piled up with ribs.

'It was the first time I've had to do everything by myself. Usually Bill does a lot of it. Still we managed all right in the end.'

I asked where the sheep came from as they had no flock of their own.

'Oh,' Irene laughed, 'Bill went out hunting yesterday. Here – have some more.'

No more snow had fallen since the day after Christmas Day but the sequence of thaw during day time and severe freezing at night made the trail to the road impassable.

'I was stuck out here for several days last winter, even with four-wheel drive,' Bill continued and poked at the fire. 'This soil is really something pretty special. Everybody and their uncle goes up and down that track, all of Irene's relations from over there.

'It's best to use that route out over that pasture. Once that snow gets packed down it's all right.'

With an early departure it was along this route that I had

managed to get down to the road two or three times and then on to the trading-post at Ganado.

About a half a mile along the road towards Ganado Lake, not far from the Mason's hogan, I had seen an abandoned truck a few hundred yards away from the road, on a trail leading out to the ridge. It turned out to be the truck belonging to the husband of an old lady who appeared at the house that morning.

She had sat near the door by the corner of the fireplace, half-turned away from Bill, Irene and myself. It seemed that her husband's truck had got stuck in the snow and now with the battery completely flat the vehicle was totally immobile.

A strange stop-and-go conversation went on for a while between Bill and the old lady, entirely in Navajo. I was unable to follow this interesting dialogue. After some time the old lady, wearing plastic 'see through' overshoes as some protection for her lightweight shoes and white socks, got up, and throwing a few more staccato phrases at no one in particular, left.

'You know,' Bill said, when the door was closed, 'I've been pulling that fella's truck out for four straight winters now. The boys have already been over there last week and towed him out. Now he's done it again.

'He's a funny old fella. When I sent the boys over there he says he wants me to come over and do it. His wife says he only wants me to pull him out and take him up to the service station and get his battery charged.

'Well,' I told her, 'I'm going to Phoenix, Flagstaff, Window Rock, Gallup and everywhere today. She thinks because she found me in the house I'm going to be lying around all day.

'Have some more mutton. There's plenty of potatoes too you know. We Navajo would live on this all the time if we could.

'Yes sir, the more fat on this mutton the better. You sometimes see Navajos cut away the lean meat and just eat the fat.' Bill chewed away at the fat on his rib.

'That's right,' Irene continued, 'if it hasn't got plenty of fat they just don't like it.'

Trying not to betray my apprehension and not looking too close at the huge rib I gnawed dutifully and mumbled something sympathetic.

'That old lady that was here the other day – she was saying how come the tribal government didn't give her a house like this one. She thought they'd given us all this.

'Well, I told her, I said "Here, we're paying through the nose for this place." Some of these people are so used to getting stuff free they think people like us got some kind of special treatment. Nearly all our money goes on the mortgage for this house. We can't afford many of those things that a lot of people get who don't go out to work.

'You know all those pick-up trucks? How do these young people get them? Well, most of the time their parents or grandparents buy them for those kids.

'A lot of families get a considerable sum of money in the welfare cheques. The older people, well, they are living in a hogan, no electricity, no gas, just like it's always been – so there are no overheads. Maybe they have sheep and cows too. When they get their cheques they buy all sorts of things. Crazy things they don't really need.

'They pay for a lot of those trucks. My aunt over there – the other side of the valley, when she sells one of her rugs she gets maybe a thousand dollars, perhaps more. She's a really good weaver. Every time she sells a rug she buys her son or other members of the family a new pick-up. Well, at least for her son she used to buy a new one but he smashed them up all the time – so she only replaces them with used ones now. But you see it's like that all the time for some of The People.'

Inside the house it had become overwhelmingly hot and I went outside to revive and breathe freely again. Shadows cast by the moon fell across freezing snow. Soft squelching and impossibly sticky during the middle part of the day, the ground underfoot was frozen rock hard. The valley bathed in that peculiar cold light of the starry sky.

A dog yapped down towards Wood Springs, a sound which struck me with the sharpness of all the other things around me. The snow glistened as though it were artificial and the ice cracked loudly as I trod between the frozen ruts. The night was brittle and raw-edged, but beautifully pure.

Returning to the house I glimpsed smoke wisping up from the hogan chimney, inside Fatso still muttered to himself as the last of the logs fell into ash.

The heat of the room and the coffee made me suddenly feel tired. I had the ache of an emotional and physical battering.

Events and confidences of the family were being poured into me and my senses whirled.

Irene offered me a wooden toothpick and then went on talking.

'When The People were collected up to begin the walk to Fort Sumner my grandfather's grandmother, his mother's mother, was among them.

'Well, as you know, there were soldiers guarding the Navajo. It was their job to keep everybody moving and to stop people running off. You know if the old people couldn't keep up the soldiers shot them sometimes. During the march one of these soldiers takes a shine to this lady and he sort of takes her off into the trees every day on their own. One day this soldier is lying down with his head in the lady's lap and he asks her to fish something out of his ear. Maybe it's wax or something, anyway there's something in there.

'So, the lady takes this little pointy stick and instead of cleaning out his ear, while he's lying there she jabs it right into his ear drum.

'The soldier starts screaming around with the pain and while he's like this, my grandfather's grandmother, she runs off through the trees – and keeps on going. She escaped completely so she never did get to Fort Sumner with the other Navajos.'

It was Yiska Damiigo, Saturday. Leaning from his truck cab window the big man spoke rapidly in Navajo to Bill who stood filling the tanks of his blue pick-up before we drove out to Klagetoh. In a strong clear morning light the general store and the gas station were a scene of activity. The isolated store tucked against the foot of the bluffs six miles west of Ganado marked the meeting of two major roads running across the reservation. The big man had finished speaking and repositioned his high crowned brown hat with its generous plume of spotted feathers and put the truck into a tight tyre-screeching U-turn to speed back down the highway towards Steamboat Canyon.

Bill finished 'gassing up' and got back into the truck.

'He says there's a ceremony tonight. A big one. A lot of people coming from all over the reservation. It's going to be over there.' Bill pointed out to the gently sloping land a little to the north of the abrupt mass of Sunrise Mesa. Snow covered the broad pastures sweeping north and west, peppered with a small cluster of hogans a mile or more from the crossroads.

'We'll come on down about ten-thirty tonight and see what's happening. Maybe it will be all right for you to watch,' Bill said, swinging the truck out and away from the buzz of vehicles outside the store.

Sunrise Mesa, a flat-topped ridge, lay on our right as we turned south along the base of its cliffs striped with horizontal bands of reds, pinks and ochres. The fog had lifted and beneath a clear blue sky the high plateau glowed.

'See that place?' Bill pointed past me to a small number of shacks surrounded by ragged bits of fencing. A hogan stood off to one side and grazing land sloped to the road from the foot of the mesa cliffs.

'That's the bootleg place I mentioned to you once before. That's Rabbit Scratch.'

I remembered Bill speaking of that place and another well-known location where Navajo bought illicit booze, the one called Black Cat, back by the bridge at Ganado.

'Translated literally from Navajo it's really Rabbit Skin,' Bill continued. 'There used to be a Hopi trader who came down to this area. He always came down over Sunrise Mesa. I don't know why but one day these Navajos ambushed him and killed him. They killed his mules and donkeys too. That place over there is where they killed the Hopi, his name was Rabbit Skin.'

We passed Sunrise Springs trading-post, a low wooden building set back from the road, nestled against the shade of cottonwood trees, and a few miles further on at Greasewood took an unpaved track east. Crossing the Colorado Wash we moved up over a high piñon and juniper-covered ridge in the general direction of Klagetoh where I hoped to meet Philip Evans, Rebecca Martgan's father, an old man living alone with his sheep and goats.

Along the horizon to the east were the sharp humps of the Lukachukai Mountains, a purple band forming a natural boundary between Arizona and New Mexico. Busy jays and laconic crows flew among the bush on either side of the trail as we moved into a covering of low misty cloud. Here the mud had remained frozen and the truck bumped along at a good speed through an area only sparsely populated by Navajo and sheep. When I made reference to the lack of people Bill shrugged and said there were probably hogans just over the hill.

'Over the hill' or 'just over there' were Navajo terms of distance I had learned to accept with caution. In my own experience 'over there' ranged from a quarter of a mile to anything up to forty miles – or more.

Completing the circuitous route of about thirty miles we entered Klagetoh from the west, then turned south for a further two miles along the paved highway leading to Wide Ruins and Chambers and then carefully began to negotiate a rugged trail meandering through piñon-covered hills in the general direction of south-west.

Philip Evans' place lay somewhere out at the end of this old wagon trail and now that the low mist had burned off, the sun began to thaw the frozen dark red earth. Although the soil around Klagetoh was for the most part lighter than the sticky clay around Bill Draper's home the trail was interrupted occasionally by large puddles of water and boggy sinks.

We passed only one visible collection of hogans a short distance from the narrow trail, as the truck pulled itself over the low bluffs with eight-cylinder determination. Two miles further on we forked right across rising ground along a drier trail and covered another two or three miles before cutting west again over the crest of a small hill. Before us lay a great shallow basin of land surrounded by low escarpments fractured by small canyons and sandy screes.

'The old boy lives way over there,' Bill shouted above the increased noise of the engine as the lower gears were abruptly changed to plough through a muddy stretch. He nodded his head towards the farthest side of sage-covered expanse. 'That's his place.'

Almost invisible in the far distance, against the sheltering backdrop of the western rim I could just make out the square form of a log cabin.

'I don't see his horse anywhere near the house,' Bill yelled and I felt the back end of the truck slide round for a moment, then hit hard ground and bounce back into line.

'See his horse?'

The cabin was difficult enough to make out from that distance, let alone a horse, and I marvelled again at Navajo eyesight.

The blue uncluttered sky blazed over the sunlit basin. We paused for a moment while Bill got out and scanned the landscape for signs of life.

With the engine stopped I listened to the silence. Dry grass and brush were streaked gold in the sun of high altitude, and the sweeping view seemed to be held in peaceful sleep.

Bill was silent. He had seen nothing between us and the rims. 'The sheep are still corralled,' he said as we came closer to the cabin. 'It's late for them to be still penned up.'

We came on slowly across the sage to the cabin and stopped in front. The door was padlocked on the outside and there were no signs of life. The sheep were, as Bill had said, still corralled and a little way off a bobtailed black dog rose from the ground and stood watching us.

The sheep milled around at our approach the neck-bells of the leaders rattling dully. Sensing no real threat the dog remained relaxed, its body taking on the movement of a cautious tail wag even though the tail, the normal canine barometer of mood, was absent.

'That's strange,' Bill said looking at the ground constantly. 'The animals haven't been out today, they've been corralled since last night. The old man must have ridden off somewheres. Maybe he's gone down to the trading-post at Klagetoh or Wide Ruins.' We scouted around looking for signs of the trail that Philip Evans must have taken out from the cabin but Bill found only a few hoof prints made the day before.

'Maybe the horse was tethered some way off from here but there should be boot-marks about the cabin.'

'You can see some but they weren't made this morning.'

I remembered Rebecca's light-hearted remark about the likelihood of my being left herding the sheep while her father went off drinking. The old man continued to live as he had when a boy but now with the guile of old age and the comparative security of a good well-bred flock of sheep, his one apparent weakness was a love of a good drink when the opportunity presented itself, and the behaviour resulting from this enthusiasm eventually resulted in husband and wife living apart.

Old Mrs Evans, a typically strong-minded and independent Navajo woman of the older ways had decided some years back that she would not tolerate the drinking habits of her husband any more and moved to a place of her own at Klagetoh. There, living a quiet well-ordered restful life she spent the summers weaving and collecting the particular plants that produced the natural dyes for her wool.

The old couple still met when Rebecca, their daughter, drove out from Window Rock and took her mother and the children out to vist their solitary grandfather. Now and again the whole family would butcher a sheep or occasionally a steer and have quite a feast out at the cabin.

Bill cast around a while longer in search of recent tracks but found nothing. I felt some disappointment at not meeting the old man as this visit was intended as an introduction from which, according to Rebecca, would be established an arrangement for me to stay and perhaps learn of her father's life and the ways of Navajos of his generation in that area.

'Well, he sure as hell has gone off somewhere. We've come a long way for nothing,' Bill climbed back into the truck and turned on the ignition.

'Maybe he's ridden off for a drink or to collect his welfare cheque.'

'We'll take that other trail there,' Bill pointed out across the sage to the north.

'Maybe we will pick up his tracks that way.'

Less used than our incoming trail the way was drier and rose gradually for about a mile to a low knoll and a protective cluster of low junipers around a small cabin and assorted paraphernalia of another of the family's sheep camps.

Bill got out again and looked intently at the trail leading away over the rise.

'I think he went down that way – back towards Klagetoh. There's only been one horse through here and that must be the old man. Anyway we better make tracks ourselves back to Ganado – he could be gone anywhere.'

We drove up out of the basin through patches of frozen snow lying in the shadows. As the sun moved up and through the blue dome the frozen earth moistened into dark stains.

'You see that boy moving those goats through the piñon?' Bill had picked out some movement off the trail to our left some way ahead. I could just see a line of animals disappear into the shadows and then re-emerge into a clearing where they began to graze, some standing on their hind legs to reach the lower branches of the juniper.

The boy kept to the edge of the small space watching our progress down the trail.

'I used to be like that when I was his age. Out all day herding the sheep and goats. You think a lot out there on your own. It's quiet. You see a lot of things, small things.

'Around late morning, noon – you let them sheep rest up and then move them on to feed later in the afternoon. Sometimes I would be with my brothers and sisters but more often I'd herd on my own.'

The small Navajo boy stood still among the trees watching us go by through the bars of sun and shade while the three or four attendant foxy-faced dogs scratched disinterestedly and lay panting.

'You like this country, eh? You see the people the way they are up here, some things don't change very much. You've got no worries when you're herding sheep.'

Bill always made reference to the simplicity of sheep herding with some tone of irony. Often he would point out some figure riding along the rims or through the piñon behind a herd.

'That's the life we all had once, everything was simple then. You know there's still a lot of kids who would rather herd sheep than go to school. Look at me always having to watch over my shoulder – trying to work out who is gonna pull the rug out from under me. Shoot; sometimes I wish I could have me some good animals and land. Politics, I guess you get enough of it too. Us Navajo have a hell of a time these days telling which way is up.'

At Klagetoh we checked for signs of the old man at his wife's spring and summer house but without success. It seemed, after passing by the Klagetoh trading-post, that he must surely have ridden south to Wide Ruins and we carried on along the black top road and over the frosted ridges back towards Ganado.

The Navajo strove to balance in the back of the lurching pick-up while swinging the stiff hoop of his lariat. Running ahead of the truck, pounding through the rough brush-covered strip of land bordering the road was the bull. We had come over the final crest before dropping to the junction of the Ganado to Window Rock road.

Another truck had pulled off the road in the sage on the left side and blocked the bull's run down the hill towards the junction. On foot were four or five other men and boys trying to corner the massive animal.

Bill jammed on the brakes and the truck powdered the earth as we ripped into the sloping verge.

'Hey, that's my brother-in-law. That bull must have travelled some way – he lives way down there over the hill.' Bill nodded in the direction of Hubbell's trading-post to the west.

'I guess they could do with some help.' He got out and turned the wheel hubs and locked the truck into four-wheel drive.

The loop had gone wide of its mark and the racing truck had stopped. The middle-aged Navajo stood recoiling his rope and watching the bull. It had stopped thirty yards off, its flanks heaving, saliva drooling from its mouth, an enormous wild eye stared from the half-turned head. For some time the chase had gone through the shallow gullies and low brush the great power of the bull always a threat, always scattering the men and boys when cornered, its horned head alert above the heavily muscled shoulders.

Now the Indians were in a position to use the truck to use its bulk and speed against the bull. In cunning and instinct the animal had the advantage, its tremendous size inhibiting anything less than caution. One of the men climbed into the back of our truck carrying an inch-thick manilla rope. The bull had managed to get past both the group on foot and the parked truck at the gateway and now trotted along the inside of the wire fence bordering the road.

Bill shouted in Navajo up to the rope-thrower in the back and the truck roared through the gate and we began the chase. At first the animal stopped and watched from a distance of fifty yards. Then as we battered through the sage and stunted pine it doubled back at a run. The ground was heaped up in earthen waves and ridges, the truck rolling and pitching its wheels cutting away gravel and roots.

Keeping a straight and converging course with the bull Bill drove the truck like a fury through the brush. I looked back through the cab rear-window and saw the Navajo with the rope almost flung out whenever the truck hit a gully. He was desperately gripping the side panels of the pick-up while trying to squat on the wheel arch, the rope loop between his teeth.

The truck spent as much time in the air as on the ground – leaping from one ridge to another, bucking, dipping and rearing in pursuit. On a rim the bull suddenly swung away to its left, our right, and Bill wrenched the wheel round hard and we roared into a collision course with the huge animal. Even if the man in the back manages to get the loop over the bull's head, I thought, what then? I saw no way that the bull would suddenly stand still in meek submission. What I did see in my mind was the Navajo roper being torn from the truck and dragged into oblivion.

Both our heads hit the roof of the cab when we plunged abruptly down a sharp incline to a shallow dry wash. Bill struggled like a madman to throw the truck into a lower gear the engine screaming, gravel and mud spraying everything, the roper flailing on his back, his boots to the sky.

Like some mythical monster the bull came over the edge of the gully snorting and red-eyed, its monumental genitalia swinging in wild pendulum rhythm.

Bill kept straight on, attempting to cut across the bull's route of escape, to halt it in its tracks. Stones were hitting the underside of the vehicle like gun shots and Bill was yelling with the excitement and I shouted in unison trying hard not to hit the cab roof too often. Both animal and vehicle were committed to their line of travel, the incline and momentum discouraging any change of direction.

'That sucker sure knows when to move,' Bill bellowed over the incredible din of the descent.

'Boy if we hit him – that's some hamburger!'

We reached the bottom of the gully almost together, the bull on a dead run, the truck on two wheels. By inches the bull missed the fender and passed in a blur of hair, saliva and dust. The animal scrambled up the other side of the wash as Bill jammed on the brakes and in the back the roper was slammed one more time against the tailgate. He must by that time have been battered black and blue but he picked himself up grinning, the rope lying in disarray, his hat blown away into the brush some way back.

Framed by the juniper at the top of the slope the brown bull stood staring back at the truck, its breath pulsing out in gusts of white steam. The Navajos scattered through the brush calling to each other in the raw winter air, and the sounds of their voices seemed tiny after the monstrous clatter and roar of the truck.

'Well, I guess they'll have to try and herd that animal back by some means, they're not going to catch it this way, that's for sure.'

Bill drove back up the road where his in-laws thanked him for trying and looked disappointedly over at the bull now wandering off at leisure among the trees.

'Hey, some hamburger that fella,' Bill said laughing and we drove back home out past Ganado Lake where the snow lay untouched beneath a low thick mist.

That night it was freezing hard as we went down to the ceremony at Sunrise Mesa. It was after ten-thirty when we arrived, the moon was up above the eastern ridges and the stars hung in ice-bright hordes.

On the snow-covered ground surrounding the hogans and remadas were lines of parked trucks. A steady stream of vehicles trundled in from the road, their headlights picking up the sparkle of the compressed snow along the track.

Bill parked on the perimeter of the gathering and went off towards the columns of sparks flying from several fires burning in the area in front of the main hogan. There were probably a couple of hundred Navajo attending the ceremony judging from the number of vehicles, all of whom might not welcome the presence of an Anglo. I felt apprehensive as a result of these thoughts and sat very still inside the dark cab of the truck while Navajos continued to arrive – emerging from the shadows and crossing through the beams of the headlights towards the fires.

'It's O.K. for you to be present at the ceremony, but you're not allowed to have cameras or anything like that.' Bill climbed back into the cab for a moment and banged the circulation back into his hands.

'I tell you that's some mean cold out there, by golly.

'I saw the head guy in charge he says it will be O.K. but stick close to me, some of these fellas really get liquored up. That place over there, the other side of those trucks,' Bill pointed to an open-topped enclosure with brush walls and illuminated slightly from inside where a fire crackled.

'In there the dancers prepare themselves. They put on their costumes and masks and nobody else is allowed to see them while that's going on. They become sort of gods through masks, they see the world through the eyes of the mask as a god. These are the Yeis. For the Navajo the Yeis represent very important gods. All Navajo children are usually initiated into ceremonial ways at the Yeibechai, the Night Way ceremony. I guess they're between about seven and thirteen years of age, and the boys and girls have this little ceremony around the eighth day of the Yeibechai which lasts for nine days. By the way, tonight is the last night, the night when the teams of Yeis sing and dance.

'These kids, they have to do special things. Two men selected by the medicine man, one wearing a black mask and one a white mask carry out special procedures and show them that the Yeis are really human at the end of these rites by taking off their masks. Then each child in turn has to put on the mask and is told to remember the god people and not to tell any other person who hasn't been initiated what they've seen.

'Maybe some have had that ceremony over there yesterday or even tonight. Let's get going.'

We came out from the darkness into a clearing lined with people. The space stretched from the dancers' preparation enclosure at its north end for about forty yards south to the door of a good-sized hogan. Here, wrapped in a red and black blanket sat the woman patient for whom the Night Way ceremony was being performed. At the edges of the clearing the Navajo stood in close ranks on hard packed snow. The polished ice surface reflected a single electric light hanging high above the hogan and the yellow and orange glow of the three or four wood fires around the edges of the clearing.

The temperature was well below freezing point and we edged our way towards the crackle and warmth of burning juniper logs. Faces, like the pressed snow underfoot, picked up the glow and flickering light from the fires, features appearing and disappearing separate from the dark anonymous mass of their bodies. Even close to the fire I could feel the cold beginning to penetrate my feet and back.

'Some guy said that they have had six teams of Yeis performing already.' Bill was hunched against the cold his parka hood pulled well forward as he scanned the far side of the clearing for familiar faces.

'Every man and his uncle is here tonight I guess,' he said and called out to a heavy-set figure with long hair hanging from below a wide brimmed black stetson.

'You know this fella,' Bill said to me, 'this is Harry, Harry Shandi, Irene's brother.' I was introduced as the guy from England writing about the family.

Harry looked up towards the hogan and pulled his collar tighter around his neck.

'One of my guys hasn't turned up yet. He better get here pretty damn quick we're gonna have to be out there in a little while.'

Harry Shandi led a team of Yeis dancers and they were to compete with the others that night.

'This is a big ceremony, these teams they come from all over, the next one is from down round Fort Wingate. Some are from Fort Defiance and Round Rock. I guess you're beginning to see what us Navajos are really like.'

The cold was biting, raw, even with the fire. Inside the hogan the medicine men were singing and had been for hours. One drummed on an upturned sacred woven basket, the chant rising and falling, its repetition creating a form of mental hypnosis.

From the shadows of the remada and the dark edge of the clearing came the two lines of dancers, led by a tall old man. He wore ordinary clothes and no doubt played the part of the director who would return to the edge of the clearing once the dancers were placed in two parallel rows a yard apart in front of the hogan. The only sounds now were the crackling from the fire and the small muted bells attached to the wrists and ankles of the dancers. Each of the figures wore a mask which did not disguise the fact that one row of dancers was made up of young Navajo girls, the other of taller and much older men.

As the dancers held their stationary positions a sudden icy gust of air threw orange sparks high into the air and across the roof of the hogan. From her sitting position at the door of the hogan the woman patient rose and, walking down the lines of dancers she sprinkled each person with sacred corn from a flat coiled basket. She gave them her blessing and returned to her seat.

Like glass the frozen snow gleamed with the dancing bands of light thrown out by the fires. It was unbelievably cold, but except for breech-cloths the men were naked, their skin painted with white clay.

For a few moments the small noises from the surrounding Navajos died away and then on a high note the chant began. Moving forward in a shuffling movement the two lines passed before the seated woman and then turned directly away from the hogan towards the east following the pattern of a narrow extended oval.

Each Yei carried a sprig of spruce in one hand and a gourd rattle in the other, their faces covered with a complete hood mask of painted buckskin punctured by small holes for the eyes and mouth. Around the neck of each was a large wreath of green spruce twigs – vivid against white clay-painted torso. At the waist each Yei wore a wide belt lavishly studded with silver and turquoise. Most wore Ketohs, the heavy bracelets and neck-laces of turquoise and silver.

Across the torso, passing diagonally from the right shoulder to the left side of the waist, was the strap of a small leather pouch fringed and decorated with silver rosettes or conchos. The short skirts or kilts of the male dancers were variously coloured and tied to by a short decorative sash. The skin of a silver fox hung at the back from the belt, the tail of the fox reaching a little below the calves of the dancer. Black socks reached to just below the knees and on the feet were soft tan-coloured Navajo moccasins, the uppers made of deerskin, the soles of rawhide, the ankle-high footwear fastened with a single silver concho disc.

By comparison with the male Yeibechai dancers, the females appeared petite, almost birdlike in stature. The young women all wore their long black hair loose to the lower part of their backs, their faces concealed by blue and white painted frontal masks, again with quite small apertures for eyes and mouth. Long flounced velveteen skirts were held at the waist by red,

white and black woven belts, and above these the girls wore
long-sleeved blouses ornamented with silver buttons. Skirts
were a rich purple, the blouses soft chestnut browns and pine
greens. Silver and turquoise earrings and necklaces jingled with
their movements, the silver catching the light of the fires. Like
the men deerskin moccasins were worn, but instead of black
socks the young women's calves and ankles were bound in the
traditional heavy white bandaging used in the past by Navajo
women for travelling but now only for ceremonies. Heavy
turquoise and silver bracelets covered the wrists and in their
white clay-painted hands each dancer held a small sprig of
spruce.

Piercing the iced air the falsetto notes of the chant rose with
the scent of juniper and showers of sparks into the ink-blue sky
above Sunrise Mesa.

My feet were beyond cold and I remembered the limping
Archie Francis. I watched, mesmerized, the slow dance of the
Yeibechai, fascinated by the white painted skin of the near-
naked men in the god masks. How were they able to perform?
The slow shuffling movements of the dance would not keep
them warm, the feet barely left the ground, the body and arms
were practically rigid. Some like myself were three feet from the
flames of a fire and still shivered violently with the cold.

I could detect neither shivers nor goose-pimples on the bare
torsos, arms or legs or any other indication that the men or
women felt the cold. Wrapped in every piece of warm clothing I
had brought to Arizona I was still frozen and yet they were
dressed for summer on a freezing January midnight, six and a
half thousand feet above sea-level.

'That white clay the dancers put on before they come out is a
protection against the cold.' Bill spoke from the depths of his
fur-edged parka hood. 'They smear it all over their skin and it
acts like a sort of insulation.'

I looked hard again at the figures whipped by freezing gusts
of wind and slowly dancing on snow. It seemed unlikely that
such a thin layer of clay, partially transparent at that, would
afford any real protection. If it did we could have used a
bucketful right there and then.

Rising and falling, blown with the wind, the Chant of the
Yeis was deadened and absorbed by surrounding darkness.

More juniper boughs fuelled the fires with sudden bursts of light, the flames biting into the dry shredded bark. Faces suddenly etched in sharp contrast of light and dark flickered in masklike exaggeration before softening into the black shadows.

Beyond the dance space within the intimacy of the starlit dark young men and women began shy new relationships, teased each other and explored fully the accepted inclinations of sexual play, the clan lineage of prospective partners carefully checked among friends and acquaintances. No person may marry within his own or his father's clan, and the Navajo reaction towards the violation of this is as severe as that towards witchcraft.

Occasional yells and shouts of euphoria broke through the darkness and labyrinth of parked pick-ups, the squeals and laughter of girls testifying to their social emancipation.

'I guess the bootleggers are doing some business tonight. Black Cat and Rabbit Scratch, those fellas never miss a do like this. You know some of these fellas will line up to get a drink or drive off the reservation to Gallup and bring it back here. If they run out of booze, heck, they'll get in their trucks and drive all the way back and get some more.' Bill nodded towards a figure lying unconscious on his side at the edge of the dance space.

The Navajo, probably about thirty years old, lay on packed snow. He wore a pair of thin trousers and a shirt half in and half out with a short light unbuttoned denim jacket. The western high-heeled boots on his feet were caked in ice and his bare head rested on a crooked arm flat on the polished snow. His hair flicked occasionally in the wind, but that was the figure's only movement I had seen since we had arrived.

'Isn't he going to freeze?' I asked. Bill shrugged. 'Yeah, unless his friends take him away. He doesn't feel anything right now. But sometimes they die.'

Quite a number of the Navajo men around us were clad only in light shirts, jackets and jeans. All wore big hats but few wore gloves or buttoned their jackets to the neck. When I remarked about this Bill carried on.

'Well, a lot of these guys have spent their lives herding sheep in all kinds of weather, winter and summer – since they were five or six years old. They're goddam tough, they wouldn't have that many clothes anyway probably. Yeah, I was like that out in all weathers on the mesa. Look at me now – got a desk job, not so tough any more.'

In the past Navajo babies were often plunged into the snow as a way of training their bodies to adjust to extreme changes of temperature – the beginning of a hardening and toughening of their stamina and physique for a lifetime's relationship with the harsher side of nature. Now, such conscious preparation for a life out of doors or for the boys' warrior responsibilities probably no longer exists, but the need for children to help herd from an early age to a large extent makes such physical adaptability natural.

Above the murmur of the watchers and the yelps of the younger Navajos beyond the circle of light, the singing continued. Each man, each girl strove to pitch their voices correctly and to move their bodies and feet in the manner prescribed by rigid religious tradition.

Each group would sing the same songs, the subtle variations of tone listened for carefully, a deviation or fault a mark against their skill as ceremonial performers.

As suddenly as it had begun the chant finished and the two lines of masked figures, six in each, walked from the lighted space past us to the remada of oak branches. The men and young women passed within four or five feet of our place near the fire, their silence accentuating their aura of another world, their sacred world.

Ordinary human beings for the Navajo are the Earth Surface People and those possessing immortality, great power and mystery are the Holy People.

From the creation of the world the Holy People – also called First People – went about the business of creating order and setting out the limits of the Navajo land. It became the task of First Man to create light and the stars, sun and moon by First Woman, the intended arrangement of the stars being foiled by Coyote who, regarded as a trickster in Navajo mythology, scattered the stars in disarray across the heavens.

Monsters emerged from the dark underworld of evil and began to kill the Earth People, unchecked until the Hero Twins, the off-spring of Earth Changing Woman and Sun and Water, brought war upon the monsters, eventually slaying these killers of the Earth People.

It is these Hero Twins, Monster Slayer and Born-of-Water, who are represented in almost all the Navajo ceremonials and now breathing heavily they passed before me into the darkness. Monster Slayer, Born-of-Water, then a barrel-chested figure whose spruce wreath collar hissed with the wind. Then came Fringed Mouth followed by Hunch Back and Black God and Water Sprinkler. These deities and the Sun and Changing Woman are amongst the most important of the Holy People and of these only Changing Woman is considered eternally of a kind disposition. Others of many roles and degrees of importance are sometimes fickle, untrustworthy, tricksters and beings who offer both good and bad. They help create a wary balance between the Earth People and the Holy People, between the certain and uncertain, a reminder of their need to be alert to the forces of the universe in which they live, to be propitiated in the defence of a good life. Through the chants and ceremonies one acknowledges the other. The chants, more commonly called 'Sings', reassure the Navajo of their beliefs.

'It's for insanity or paralysis or something very serious like going blind or deaf that the Yeibechai ceremony is held.' Bill spoke against the increasing cold and draughts cutting through the groups of Navajos around us.

'The woman by the hogan door, she's the patient, it's for her. I don't know what's wrong but I guess she and her relatives are going to try everything to get cured. Other curing chants are for different sickness like skin problems, heart trouble and when people get very depressed and sort of nervous. A lot of those types of problems and others like snakebite and stuff are cured by the Bead Chant, Mountain Way, Shooting Chant and the Windways.

'All these curing ceremonials like the other chants have to be paid for by the patient and the relatives. These dancers, each team will get a sheep. They reckon there's about nine teams here tonight and that's only part of it all because all these relatives that come from all over they have to be fed too. The medicine men they cost a lot for a thing this big – some beef maybe, quite a lot of dollars and other things.

'This is the last night of the nine-day ceremony, these medicine men will sing in the hogan until the sun comes up – then it is finished.'

Bill had not spoken of the sand paintings, that part of the curing ceremony most associated with Navajo religion, and perhaps did not want to.

During the nine-day Yeibechai ceremony the medicine man and his assistants usually make four Sand Paintings, perhaps more correctly called Drypaintings. Finely ground minerals, charcoal, pollen and corn meal form the colours while the sand is usually used only for the background, spread upon the hogan floor. The colours are applied by letting the pulverised materials trickle out through the thumb and index fingers of the hataali and his assistants to create a design representing mythological figures and stories of the Holy People.

Dry paintings can vary in size from designs only a foot square and taking an hour to make up to enormous designs requiring perhaps twelve or fifteen men working all day on an area twenty feet in diameter. The paintings made on consecutive days are intricate and stylized, the format of the design handed down exactly from one hataali to the next. Very few minor variations are acceptable and the main colours of black, white, yellow and blue symbolise the cardinal directions – white is east, yellow west, north is black and south blue.

When completed the patient is seated facing east in the centre of the Drypainting and the hataali, by placing his hands upon areas of the painting and then against the patient's body, transforms power from the deities to the patient. Sickness or evil has become absorbed into the sand and this is taken out and ceremonially buried when, at the end of the day, the painting is destroyed.

Still observing and acknowledging relatives and clan members, Bill said, 'No matter how many churches you see on the reservation nearly all Navajo believe in the old religion. The medicine men are very important to us, even though a lot of the old ways are gone. That's Water Sprinkler out there or maybe Talking God, I'm not sure, that young fella out front.'

A team of dancers had come out from the brush corral and formed the two rows in front of the hogan. Bill indicated a young boy who seemed to perform somewhat like a jester. The boy was also masked and danced in front of the two lines of Yeibechai dancers, advancing towards and retreating from the oncoming chanting figures as if to make them stumble. Falsetto voices kept up the chant's exacting rhythm, its cadences bring back the sharp attention of the people.

Perhaps somewhere between forty and forty-five years of age the woman's face was composed and attractively dignified. Her face seemed too unmarked, too tranquil to hide the beginnings of severe sickness or insanity and she had moved along the lines of Yeis with such poise that the sprinkling of the sacred corn pollen appeared to be the benediction of nobility.

Watching her I felt a great sadness. For her and her family this dramatic conclusion of the Night Chant was of the greatest importance.

Out of this ceremony, the chanting, the Drypaintings, and the prayers would hopefully come the relief she sought and I felt the sympathy of the people would join with the singing of the medicine men to invoke the compassion of the Holy People. In those moments I felt that all the prayers must be answered.

'We'd better make a move. It's somewhere around one-thirty, and this will go on till dawn. The medicine men have to sing until then but I'm frozen, let's go.' Bill started up the pick-up and reversed out of the ranks of parked vehicles. With blankets and without, young Navajo couples hunched against the sides of trucks earnestly making use of the dark.

A truck roared out of the sage, bounced on to the packed snow and spun like a top, its headlight beams catching many of the night's intimacies unawares. Figures moved quickly away into yet colder shadows.

'That sucker is gonna get his butt shot off if he hits anything. Crazy fool. They don't care, some of these young studs. Hell, their grandmother's probably gave 'em money and a truck. After a few drinks they go wild. Some of them start to forget what all this is about. Maybe they've seen too many movies down at Gallup and Flagstaff.'

We moved away from the circle of light and the singing and skidded round towards the road to the south. Our lights picked out the startled looks of a couple lying in a snow-and-ice-filled ditch obviously defying the cold in single-minded and enthusiastic copulation.

'What did I tell you, boy, these young Navajos are tough, see them go!' Bill laughed and we bumped on and back to the road.

The vision of those two Navajo rolling in the snow with such determination exposing their flesh to the elements made mine shrivel at the very thought and my legs involuntarily clamped themselves together like the jaws of a vice and I laughed my head off. 'Hey, they weren't even wearing white clay,' I shouted back at Bill.

For the two or three days following the Yeibechai ceremony I was confined once more to the hogan in a freezing world of white. I made occasional trips to the woodpile and uncomfortable rushes to the narrow wooden sentry-box, staying as briefly as possible, quickly reading last year's news in the *Navajo Times*.

Each morning I woke to the illumination of the chimney hole and tried to deduce the mood of the weather by the colour of its space. The windowless hogan seemed at its most austere in those early hours of the morning. Black and empty of warmth the squat woodstove sat beneath its chimney pipe, a headless neck poking into the dawn.

The dust of the earth floor smelled a little of summer but the ice-topped water in the bucket by the door offered little encouragement to get up, to put some purpose to the day.

On these days and others as cold and entombing I spent the first hours in recollection, my thoughts flowing out in their own indulgent patterns, dissolving and reforming, challenging any intrusion of structure.

I became increasingly sensitive to the differences of the world in which I was now living. The perspective and viewpoints from which as an Anglo I judged the worth and manner of things and events, seemed to dissolve. Daily exposure to Navajo attitudes and thought had now formed a new but unobtrusive framework from which it was possible to recognise more easily the needs of their existence, the general pattern of their lives. It was from within the tribal circle that I often found myself looking outwards occasionally to the world from which I had come.

From the very first contact with the representatives of white America in 1846 the conflicts of the separate cultures have continued until the present day. In their homelands, regarded by whites as quite worthless until the recent discovery of valuable minerals, they have fought long and hard to remain different and to retain the form of their heritage as native Americans whose spiritual codes did not evolve in Europe.

In essence the hogan had brought me unconsciously into the inner ring of the Navajo circle and from its centre, I was now able to see the distortions and the dilemmas of choice, especially for the young. Through schooling comes still the greatest influence of white society and the imposition of its values, although tribal government may more strongly define the future direction of Navajo culture.

Centres such as the Navajo Community College at Tsaile could become the powerhouse of south-western Indian realignment through its questioning and establishment of Navajo cultural identity. One could hardly fail to notice the importance of heightening Navajo awareness within the opportunities of education constructed not for the Anglos, but for Indians.

Certainly after my brief visit to the snow-bound campus I felt quite sure that a number of positive programmes were being attempted. In these, young Navajos would need to recognise their own responsibilities in the building of strong tribal and cultural identity to generate greater awareness of wider global realities and to cope with the pressures of the surrounding Anglo culture.

Such an escalation of Navajo cultural education would be short-sighted indeed if it promoted this through isolationism or debilitating social introspection. Until such time as there is sufficient employment within the reservation a great number of young people will either begin a life-style which relies upon federal welfare benefits or seek more productive work off the reservation. It would be unfortunate indeed if administrational and economic centres were expanded or newly established on the reservation at the sole initiative of the Anglos interests.

Bill had come into the hogan and stood silhouetted against the light of the door.

'I've just come over to see if you're O.K., you've got wood and stuff. I'd better feed these damned chickens too. I don't know about those boys – I bet they forget to feed 'em most days. Porky hates that rooster. That sucker's mean – you don't need to turn your back on that guy.'

That morning I had opened my eyes to the grey light of the chimney hole with an almost feverish relief and the uncanny feeling that the hogan itself had begun to affect my moods, particularly during the hours of darkness.

Slowly warming as the grey sky lightened, I lay half-mesmerised by the chimney hole, trying to unravel the sequence of imagery – and perhaps the meaning of a dream I'd had.

It had been neither day nor night and the air was a yellow warm mist. Objects seemed illuminated from all sides, the source of light lost within the mist and beyond it.

There were no sounds but things had life. Trees with white limbs encircled a clearing within the yellow mist, its centre swept clean, the ground hard and level and pale silver sand like a sheet of glass though I could see each grain of sand separately.

I walked down the slope through the trees, their substance evaporating in my path and into the centre of the space. Ripples of shadow, like water, ran out from where I stood. It seemed I was without my real form and only my eyes had substance. I looked down to watch my feet making the ripples but there *were* no feet or legs. I felt disembodied and I floated as a single eye.

At the centre stood a dun coloured steer. It appeared gaunt but was really only an animal without surplus fat, its skin pulled tight across perfect sinew and muscle. What made the steer remarkably different was its absence of horns. From its head grew instead two pairs of antlers, each with eight points. One set grew from the normal position at the top of the skull above the ears while the other swooped forward from a position just above the eyes.

It spoke with a human voice but I could not understand its language and was increasingly embarrassed at not having legs and feet and kept looking down, somehow thinking that they might grow as the steer continued speaking. As the animal spoke it raised and lowered a hoof in turn quite rapidly and in a clockwise direction, the movement causing a muffled drumming.

For what seemed a long time the steer continued its monologue accompanied by the drumming hooves and then stopped abruptly and lay down on its side – as though dead.

I came up to the animal, its legs stretched out straight showing the underside of the hooves to be a shining glass-like material. The hide of the steer, like the grains of sand, could be seen both as a mass and as individual hairs, the skin undulating and indicating the animal was alive. Its head was propped up by two sets of antlers and one open eye mirrored mine.

I waited, looking intently at the hairs on the steer's side, the single eye watching me as though I was expected to do exactly this.

At last the steer jumped up scattering dust as it pulled its half-embedded antlers from the ground.

'Must I do something now?' I asked the steer, not expecting any response as its language was heretofore incomprehensible. I suppose surprise would have been a normal reaction to its reply in English but I could not even blink as I was without an eyelid.

'You must not look at the ground – it has not gone away,' said the steer. 'You do not have those feet which touch the ground and you see that here it is all cracked except for the narrow strip around this hogan.'

I now stood with the steer at the door of a hogan. Unlike the one in which I slept with its roof of board and tarred felt, this was of the older style, made of logs and covered with a dome of red earth.

'What you must do is walk around the hogan for a long time, as I will – but I will go the opposite way and you must touch my antlers when we pass each other.' The steer seemed agitated and impatient to begin this ceremony.

Again I was embarrassed at not having legs and feet and was reluctant to begin.

'We start now from this doorway, you go to the north and I will go around the south side.'

The steer's manner of walking was the same as the movements it made while remaining in one place – the hooves rising and falling in rotation, a continuous soft drumming into the yellow mist.

No longer was the hogan on the ground; it revolved slowly upon its own axis – a mirror image of itself grown from its base, the two parts becoming a red sphere.

'You must never fail to touch my antler in your passing, the skin of the hogan is as the skin of the ground and the skin of the air.' The steer and the eye of my self were held in rhythmic orbit, slowing at the point when I must touch the antler and then quickening away.

From a long way off I watched the eye of my self become silver wire and the antlered steer stretched into vapour, the two spinning a translucent film around the red hogan.

'It is yellow space,' the steer spoke.

'The hogan you see – it is there and it is here. Your eye is the hogan and you must hold yourself at its centre. You must touch the antler from the inside as well as the outside, the light will not make shadows nor will it warm you.'

That sudden withdrawal of heat made me very nervous and I thought it vindictive and unnecessary. Why had the steer disappeared? The hogan too had gone and that had seemed a way back – at least to something I could touch.

'The light will only let you see, it offers nothing else, it's silly to think it will.'

In the silver sand, each grain shining brilliantly, the steer held its place again, drumming its hooves softly.

I was very tired, now I had legs and feet, and I drew my finger round each toe cleaving an outline and watched the grains of sand falling back into the tiny impression.

'You should always go that way round,' the steer continued speaking but its voice gradually fading, 'and touch the antler yourself. It is your part, your part, your part, yourpart-yourpart-yourpart. . . .'

The drumming had died to a murmur with the words and I was too heavy and fell down between the grains of sand not knowing what to do.

I began to push aside each grain of sand but found that each one had suddenly become a boulder of immense size. From behind each boulder appeared the antlered steer, the hair of its back and sides now long and swept into the patterns of long grass combed by a strong wind.

The hair parted along the steer's back and I could see down into the canyon and began to climb down to where the Indians sat singing by the wash.

Cold light burned down the chimney hole and I felt unusually alone, and for a moment like the last man under the snow of the high mesas.

Bill came into the hogan and closed the door as I sat up in bed and lifted the lid of the stove. I thought I would mention the dream, still feeling exhausted by its intensity and related briefly the central matter of the antlered steer and the circling of the hogan.

'A cow in a dream is regarded as a bad omen by the Navajo. It is not a good thing.' Bill looked severe, unless I had read something in his face which really was not there, and he squeezed his nose.

'I don't know about something like that animal – or what it means. Some people are very superstitious about dreams and go to the medicine man. You know – for help to find out if there are bad influences. Things like that.'

Bill scooped up some grain from a sack by the door and went off to the chicken coop closing the door of the hogan behind him. For a while I lay wondering about the dream and Bill's response and then got up and dressed – and broke the ice on the water bucket.

It was time to leave. Weather reports prophesied more snow coming down from the north-west across Nevada and Utah – a spreading cloud belt that would probably release the bulk of its load on the Rockies but a significant portion would fall on north-east Arizona. The already bleak conditions had continued to restrict the movements of myself and the Navajos. Wood-cutting and hauling, splitting logs and keeping warm seemed to be the main concern of everyone. Smoke curled from the hogan chimneys in a silent passive landscape, and even the black crows seemed less confident, less assured in their flight over the white mesa.

There were few days left before my flight was due to leave San Francisco for England and once more the details of driving to that point eleven hundred miles away had to be dealt with. Once across the border of California I would drop down into warmer valleys, leaving the cold high mesas of Arizona and the vagaries of the reservation winter far behind me.

I said my goodbyes to the family and land, walking out to the ridge for the last time enjoying its familiarity and the quietness of the snow. From the horns of the ridge my eyes ran out to the Nazlim and Chinle valleys and however difficult, I knew that I would return to the Navajo in the spring.

In darkness, at four-thirty the next morning, I drove away from the hogan to the road, cutting a last winter trail across the frozen snow and sage brush. From Nevada the new snow clouds were moving southwards to the mountains of Arizona and as the pale dawn broke I crossed the western boundaries of the reservation. For the Navajo the winter continued; it was 'the time when the snakes sleep'.

Part 3

Spring

It was April now and I felt no real surprise that the Ganado ridge was pocked with white and the land still waited for the full flush of the Spring.

California had been sun-filled and warm. Surfers were out along the beaches waiting for the tilt of a wave.

As I began the slow climb to the Canyon de Chelly area, it was freezing in the mountains around Prescott. Large amounts of snow still filled the gullies and shadowed slopes. Through Oak Creek Canyon the ice was thick at the creek edge, the white trunks of aspens and birch matching themselves with the snow trapped in this deep mountain cleft. The sun's reflection off the ice was blinding and roads steamed with the thaw that I hoped had started earlier on the reservation.

At Flagstaff I took Highway 40 and about sixty miles further on, just past Meteor Crater, I went north into the reservation. A few miles west of Leupp the trail turned east towards Dilkon and I was into unknown territory. All this land along the south-west corner of the Navajo reservation was new to me and the prospect of further exploration gave an edge to the morning. As I followed the uncompromising unpaved road I found myself in a country of vast sweeping red uplands softened with yellow grass. As if freshly painted, the sky was clear blue and enormous.

Away from shadows of rocks or trees, the recent snow had melted into the land but the appallingly deep wheel-ruts of the trail still held frosted earth lumps and broken ice. Thrown from one gouged rut to another I drove the truck laboriously for forty miles and then after Dilkon the trail climbed slightly through Indian Wells and Bitahochi – and got worse. My earlier smugness began to fade.

Hardly an Indian visibly crossed the landscape. It appeared at times entirely vacant but I knew that Navajo families lived in those great expanses, each part of the land accounted for. What I could not see, existed. Out of all those hidden places beyond the bluffs and buttes the Navajo travelled out to the markets of Flagstaff, Winslow, Chambers and Gallup. Water had to be hauled from the tribal artesian wells and wood gathered from the piñon and ponderosa pine forests. Their business done, the families would travel back along the faint distant trails and disappear into their majestic land.

Smashed and pounded from side to side I waited for the truck to fall apart. There was no turning back now. I drove on almost rigid with the tension of physical punishment and the strain of an over-active imagination. Sometimes I was able to lose myself in the immensity of my surroundings, but the possibility of a broken axle or disintegrating steering-box haunted me.

When I reached the paved road at Greasewood, about fifteen miles from Ganado, I had driven over a hundred miles of gravel and frozen mud from Meteor Crater. I could hardly remember the thousand miles before that.

On the mesas the grass had yet to show its new growth even though the sun now warmed the earth. On the lee side of the ridge I could see my hogan, its familiar squat form against the juniper. The pastures were deeply scarred by the winter trails through the snow from the house to the road. The main track was still in a bad way but passable and I drove slowly up to Bill Draper's place with a smashed wheel-bearing.

That night I ate Navajo fry bread, chicken and rice with Bill and Irene Draper, their children and the Morgans from Wood Springs. My reinstatement among the family had been made with little realization among any of us of my three-month absence. It was almost as though I had not been away, had not flown twelve thousand miles and driven over two thousand since leaving them in January.

There was, however, one new and interesting change to the household. Arnold Youvella, Irene's oldest son by her first marriage, had come home to live with his other brothers, half-brothers and half-sisters. Irene's first husband had been a Hopi, and Arnold, half-Navajo, half-Hopi, had for the last few years been living with his grandmother at Polacca on the Hopi reservation about sixty miles west of Ganado.

Drinking among young people had become a serious problem on the Hopi mesas and Arnold had been no exception in the combination of high-spirited behaviour and general difficulties

Arnold Youvella painting his kachinas at Ganado

with the Indian police. Arnold had been put into a rehabilita-
tion programme which he had completed in a section of the
Navajo reservation and now among his family at Ganado he
had few opportunities or encouragement to drink. He earned
money by making Hopi Kachina dolls and pottery. The so-
called dolls were carved from canyon driftwood, usually very
light cottonwood roots, and were painted and dressed in the
traditional costume of Hopi ceremonial figures. At Polacca
tourists had bought whatever Kachina dolls Arnold had to sell
and with the profits, there being little else to do, he and other
young Hopi craftsmen drank heavily. On occasion they would
pool their money and go to Albuquerque, Phoenix or even San
Diego and Los Angeles.

Arnold and I shared the hogan. My presence was undoubtedly a novelty for him and I was pleased to have company
occasionally. We rearranged the general clutter and I made up
a bed alongside Arnold's against the back wall with the woodstove at our feet between us and the door.

'We would just go off and stay in a motel and have twenty-
dollar meals until the money ran out,' Arnold explained. 'Then
we'd go back to Polacca and make some more dolls. One
time I went right up to Montana. I was walking around with
snow up to my arse all the time. It didn't really suit me up
there.'

On a box near the hogan door were half a dozen small
wooden figures in various stages of carving. Knives and wood
shavings littered the floor.

'I have seven orders I have to make right now. See, this is
how I make them.'

Arnold explained his method of sawing out the basic doll
form from the cottonwood roots and then developing the more
detailed work with small knives and files. Against the hogan
wall was a stack of dry cottonwood roots, some four or five
inches in diameter while others were no more than an inch. The
larger pieces would form the bodies of the dolls while the
smaller roots were used for the arms.

'Right now there's a warrant out for my arrest in Polacca,'
Arnold lay back on his camp-bed and contemplated the hogan
ceiling for a moment. 'When I've finished the dolls I can pay off
the fine. I had the money several times before but each time I

just spent it. If I go over there and I don't have the money they'll put me in jail.

'Once I was in jail down in Winslow for four months for driving while intoxicated. I didn't want to bother my Ma but eventually they came and got me out.'

I lit the pressure lamp and it soaked the log walls again with its yellow light. Its friendly gurgling hiss made a comforting background sound, forever evocative of my life in the hogan.

'It snowed on me the other night,' Arnold mused sleepily. 'It came all ways down this chimney hole.'

Christmas memories came back. I saw the snows of December and January falling on to the stove and the icicles dripping from the hogan eaves. Surely April would not be so harsh. After the light had been turned out I lay looking up at the six-sided plate of night sky and wondered at the oddness of my situation and the circumstances of my involvement with the Navajo.

Having arrived I could hardly remember the coming – and yet on the journey I was unable to envisage its end. I slipped through the stages of adjustment from one world to the other, a metamorphosis curiously tranquil with moments of recognition like that of a familiar action or a smell that casts the mind back to a time of one's childhood.

Bill and I came down from the pine- and juniper-covered mesa. On our right the secret cracks and scarred water courses of Kin Li Chee Canyon cut into the red lands eastwards. Bill drove the blue truck at a steady forty-five to fifty, even after the paved road finished at the base of the escarpment and we began the meandering dirt road to Chinle.

Not even a single shining pocket of snow remained on the valley floor but in places the red earth showed damp dark stains. Packed down into bone-hard washboard ridges, the clay trail swept out through the open scrub lands past occasional giant molehills of earth striped brown and grey. Through the treeless undulations of the valley a wash ran with thick rippling mud water, its soapy slickness breaking away in a shallow basin near the road to form a small lake. Here, unhurried in clear sunshine the turbulent earth water settled and cleared into a pan of silver light streaked with the turquoise sky.

In a continual paroxysm of protest the truck vibrated along the road but our speed diminished neither for rut nor turn.

At Chinle we found the small community unusually quiet for a Saturday. Garcia's Trading Post was without its posse of trucks with Navajos coming and going, inspecting each other.

A little north of the bridge over the wash at the mouth of Canyon de Chelly, three children rolled and splashed fully dressed in the shallow waters running across the wide canyon floor. It was snow water but the children seemed oblivious of the cold. Weather alone wouldn't be enough reason to stop their fun.

Old Henry Draper stood in his familiar stance by the wood-pile. His hand shading his eyes, he looked out to where the goats grazed on the southern slopes of the ranch. The dogs, larger than ever, raced out to meet the truck as we pulled up into the yard. Old Henry wore a new brown legionaire's style képi and looked a lot fitter than he had in January. Garnet had gone off to Gallup to buy Easter eggs for the family.

'We had snow almost every night except last night since Christmas. Really bad winter this year.' The old man grinned and waved his hand out towards the ridge behind the hogan.

'Tommy is out there somewhere. I don't know where he went.'

The youngest of the sons, Tommy, was the only member of Henry and Garnet Draper's family that I had not met. Usually he lived with his sister down at Many Farms but this year he had spent a good part of the winter with his parents at Del Muerto.

Bill left for a meeting at Tsaile, saying that he would pick me up in two or three hours. While he attended to business of the Bureau of Indian Affairs, I was free to wander out towards the rim of Canyon del Muerto. I left Henry to his wood-chopping and struck out towards the canyon, taking the route leading to the rim above Twin Trails.

I followed a solitary line of footprints for half a mile and then lost them among the rock shelves. Although a gust of wind hissed through the branches it was warm among the juniper. In the shale screes tiny alpines were in bloom and the delicate petals of minute white flowers opened up to the sharp sunlight. Blue jays and a pair of ravens followed me down through the rocks and shattered the whispers of the wind with their calls.

The clarity of light in the mountains made trees and rocks sparkle against their precise shadows cast in slits and splashes, purple-edged on the drying earth and fissured rock. To the south-east, mare's tail clouds whirled in giant arcs and behind me in the west the sky was plain turquoise.

I soaked in the land again and basked on the rocks above the snow water pools along the bed of the small canyon. Squirrel and bird tracks etched the moist sand around the pools, the edges of which in some places held cleanly pressed tracks of deer.

Black, polished and heavy-beaked, two ravens perched on the ledge above me discussing my progress. Their plumage, the colour of peacocks' throats, some blue jays played hide and seek through the green juniper, their sickle crests alert and eyes full of mischief.

At three o'clock I turned back towards the ranch following the diminishing canyon to its modest beginning and found an old Navajo sweat house against a wall of rock shadowed by pines. The small conical structure, no more than five feet high at its apex, was constructed on inclined juniper logs with a small door opening to the east. Inside, on the north side of the door, were rocks placed in a low stack and these would have been the pre-heated rocks over which water was poured to produce the steam of ritual and physical purification.

I clambered over the last remaining ragged ledges to the cattle fence and, crossing the road, came up the track to the corrals and water trough.

Another figure, unfamiliar, was swinging an axe at the woodpile in the yard. Even when the dogs ran out the man did not look up at my approach. Coming near I called out and he turned and at first spoke in Navajo. Then he laughed and asked after the health and general welfare of the 'Queen of Britain'!

It was Tommy. 'I've been up here keeping an eye on Mom and Dad this winter. Shoot, they're gittin' too old. Well, I'm the black sheep of the family.'

I had guessed as much from the comments made by others of the family and I sensed he was regarded with both irritation and envy.

'Damn, – I could do with a little Jim Beam right now. You

don't have any with you?' Trying to gauge Tommy's mood I struck a chord of casual humour and we got along just fine.

'Hell, what is the difference between Scotch and whisky anyway?'

Tommy showed all the signs of having had a drink or two fairly recently but he was fully capable of leading into detailed enquiries.

'Hey, were you the guys up there in the tent last summer? Shoot, I saw you one day. You've been down Mexico, right? I saw that book you wrote. Francis showed me that.'

This surprised me, for although Francis had never referred to the book after its acceptance he had obviously thought it interesting enough to show to his youngest brother.

I told Tommy about the sweat house I had found in the canyon and asked him if my assumption of its use had been correct.

'Yeah, that's what it was all right. One time I was on a two-week drunk down around Fort Defiance and this guy got me to have a sweat bath.

'They was singing and everything and they want me to get all that poison out of me. I couldn't even piss, they tied a string round my cock so I wouldn't lose any water.

'Well they had sure sweated it out of me when I was done. Boy, I was so light I wanted to run and run. Then – you roll on that hot sand.

'Shoot, I drank down a cold beer straight off. Boy, I really felt good.'

We went into the little frame house where old Henry was sitting on the bed by the window sewing up his trousers.

'He won't let me do that,' Tommy rolled a fraction but caught himself. 'He sure would make me a good wife,' he laughed and paced around the tiny room.

'Sit down, sit down there on the bed, it don't matter none.'

'My Dad, he won't let anybody do anything for him . . . I don't know about him.'

The bedroom had a small woodstove in one corner and while his father finished his sewing Tommy squatted on his heels and lit the paper and shredded bark.

Rows of photographs were pinned on the walls above the old man's bed. Sons and daughters, many old and faded prints

An old sweat-house framework in Monument Valley, similar to the
one in the Canyon

punctuated with sharper images of more recent grandchildren.
Underneath the window at right angles to the old man's double
bed was Garnet Draper's single bed. The only other furniture
were a few shelves and boxes. Broken oilcloth partially covered
the earth floor.

'I was reading something the other day about the Maya
Indians.' Tommy got the fire started, stood up and continued
with an increasingly unexpected intermingling of questions and
statements.

'Yeah, they made some pretty good stuff. Are they related to
us Athabascan-speaking Indians? What those Mexican Indians like down there? Are they living like us Navajo?'

Tommy looked out of the window, 'Well, I could do with
some of their cerveza, that's good beer they have.'

I wanted to ask old Henry about the killing of the grizzly bear in the canyon years ago but being partially hard of hearing the old man wasn't too certain of my questions.

Tommy cleared the way by speaking to his father in Navajo to make sure he understood my enquiries.

Henry's eyes lit up behind his thick pebble glass spectacles. 'Oh, that bear. Yes, that bear he killed some calves.' The old man's high creaky voice came in abrupt sentences.

'It buried a calf. Pulled the dirt over it and left it there. Me and my brother went out in the canyon to hunt for it. There were other Navajos but they were off some other place in the canyon. We found that bear up on a rock just above us. I shoot that animal close up. It started shaking its head from side to side and rearing up. It took two more shots to kill it.'

The huge grizzly had, more or less, been the last of its kind seen in Canyon del Muerto and its killing was normally regarded as taboo. The Navajos had only hunted it because of its developing appetite for their livestock. Such an enormous and infrequently seen animal had caused a lot of attention in the area and after the shooting it had been photographed lying in an open buckboard. Prestigious in its size and regard by the Navajo and in particular that of Henry Draper, he presented the skin to the Presbyterian church at Del Muerto where it hung for many years – a reminder of another age.

Tommy kept saying something about killing another bear later with an axe but these interjections became either lost accidentally in the general confusion of translation or were discreetly evaded, perhaps in relation to the aspects of taboo.

Old Henry fell back on the double bed and made soft humming sounds while Tommy rekindled his own enthusiasm for all kinds of alcohol.

'I been to California too. Studied criminology over there for a while but this is my land. Shoot. They got more liquor over there – but all those people running around! Well, it didn't do me no good, no sir. I guess I'm just the black sheep. Damn. Just look at my Dad. I don't know about him.'

Tommy jumped up from inspecting the progress of the stove and checked a paper calendar hanging by the door. 'Maybe getting on for a full moon. That's when the calves come. You can tell pretty good a few days either way. Women is the same,' he said winking and pulling his red woollen hat down tightly.

Suddenly Tommy and his father became alert to something else. 'Someone's coming. Yeah, it's my Mom,' said Tommy, looking out through the kitchen window. He was excited, his movements quicker. 'Maybe she brought a few "tortillas".' He said this jokingly but only half-attempted to conceal the real expectation and concern which was cerveza, Mexican beer.

Garnet Draper came through the door, full of surprise and pleasure to see me. For a while we talked of the troubles that winter but Tommy hovered at the door nervously. It was obvious that he had made an arrangement with his mother to buy liquor for him at Gallup and he teased and prompted her trying to discover whether she had or not.

I suspected that Garnet had brought his drink but would say nothing of it in my presence. Tommy's playful good-humoured questioning had an underlying urgency and the single-mindedness of someone addicted to alcohol.

Another figure appeared in the kitchen, coming from the shadows of the little back room where Tommy slept. He was short and heavily built with dark, almost menacing, features set beneath a great wide-brimmed black hat and he had driven Garnet to Gallup and back. The looks of the man belied his nature and I later found him to be quite approachable. As the figure made his departure I noticed his limp and the action jogged an image to mind of seeing him on a couple of occasions in the summer, walking across the pastures from Del Muerto.

'Well, I tried everywhere to get those Easter eggs but they were sold out. I think I left it too late. Everybody was after them.'

Garnet glared at Tommy who was still pacing by the window. Tension between him and his mother could be felt and the humour was quickly fading from Tommy's originally light-hearted banter.

Garnet Draper retreated to the kitchen table, sat for a while and appeared to be considering the next move. She was obviously upset with Tommy's behaviour, probably more so with the embarrassment of me being a witness to the events.

Tommy, having got nowhere with his partially veiled re-quests, stomped off outside shouting something about his horses. When he had gone I joined old Garnet at the table.

'I don't know why he gets like that,' she said, stern-faced.

'Whenever that other fella is around he gets so stupid. He says that other man is staying in his room back there.'

This reference seemed to be to yet another person I had not seen or who was at that moment away from the house.

'When he's on his own with us he's all right. He chops wood and goes out early in the morning with the goats. He checks the horses and everything. As soon as anybody else comes round here all he thinks of is drinking. It makes me angry. I don't like it.'

She paused and brushed a few crumbs from the table top. 'You didn't bring your son this time? We remember him well.'

Once more the family showed its concern for us. The hints in conversation and manners indicated the relationship between myself and the family had become important. We reflected upon the bad weather and the old couple's health. Garnet had a sore throat and had been taking medicine for a couple of weeks but Henry appeared much better than of late and generally they had both managed well during the snows.

'Tomorrow morning, Easter Sunday, they're having a service at six o'clock up on the mesa. I don't know if we'll make it,' she laughed. 'It's for the Catholics and Presbyterians. They have a sunrise service every year.'

Tommy came back in and said he was going into Chinle to see some friends. Both he and his mother knew what it would be about. She said nothing, her look was enough. But he went anyway.

Bill arrived at that point and in a little while we were thundering across the Chinle Valley again towards the red bluffs of Kin Li Chee. Like iron the clay ribs of the road pounded the truck in its unfaltering speed.

Above the noise Bill related a story passed down from his grandmother and I strained my ears to hear it all.

'It seems to me,' he began, 'that my grandmother mentioned some names of people in some incident that happened over here that were sort of familiar. I don't recollect them right now but I guess it was around my great-grandmother's time.

'It was the time the Navajo were being rounded up. They put a lot of people out here in this big open valley. You see they couldn't run off anywhere without being seen by the lookouts all up on the bluffs. Those Navajo were being held there before beginning the mark to Fort Sumner.

'Anyway there used to be some wild rice growing down here and there was a group of Navajos who had moved off over there on the mesas towards Kin Li Chee Canyon and they needed to find more food. They sort of discussed the matter and decided to come down at night to get the wild rice. This one old lady with the group said there were bad signs and they shouldn't go down, it would be dangerous. Well, they decide to go down despite the old lady's warning.

'So they come down to pick the rice and move out into the valley here but pretty soon they heard shots and they're all scattered about not knowing what's happening. Then these Utes and the cavalry ride up and start shooting everybody. Only thirteen Navajo got away that night, all the rest were killed.

'Those Utes were scouts for the cavalry. Different tribes scouted against other tribes for the army. Navajo against Apache and Apache scouts against Navajo. It was quite normal practice in those days.'

When we got back to the hogan Arnold was carving his Kachina dolls by the stove, shaping legs, arms and torsos. He cut and filed, his eyes almost closed against the fine cottonwood root dust.

'It's not good for your eyes this stuff. I don't see so good anyway without my contacts.'

That was a surprise but I said nothing. Arnold continued, 'Over in Polacca,' he was hunched over the half-finished figure resting on his knee, 'I was riding some pretty wild horses. Well, they just popped out and that was that. I lost some others too. That time I only had them a couple of weeks. I'm hopeless with stuff like that.

'You know it doesn't take long to make a Kachina doll really. I could do it in a couple of days. Guess I'm lazy. No, it's not just that – but I guess a lot of it, but I like to mess around with the kids a lot. I've been away so much over in Polacca and places.

'I think the young ones, Patrick and Hank are going to do all right later on. They've got a good father. We never had no father Wayne, Chet and me when we was young. My Dad was a drunk, still is – over in Polacca. Boy he's been married about six times, he don't change none though.

'I think I'd like to build a house over here. Do everything myself.' Arnold lay back in the old green plastic-covered rocker and mused on his ambitions.

'I know my grandmother, my Mom's mother wouldn't mind. It would be O.K. The tribe give you a permit for two, three hundred logs or so and if I could get someone to draft out the plans. I'd have to have foundations and stuff.

'Yeah, I'd like to do that. Make all my own furniture too, just natural like, made out of wood like that.' Arnold pointed to the stack of cottonwood roots at the back of the hogan.

I lay on my camp-bed, occasionally reading a word or two of a book while Arnold talked on freely roaming from one aspect of his life to another.

'You know I never got really involved with any of those Hopi girls over in Polacca. If you start going around with one of them for a while she starts getting ready to marry and tells all the other girls. In Polacca everybody knows what's going on, what everybody is doing. Boy, if her parents find out you're seeing their daughter regularly they start making plans. Then, if you take off because the girl is getting too serious all those other Hopi girls get funny and won't have anything to do with you.

'Hell, it's better not to have anything to do with them. If you do anything over there on the mesa, you get drunk or do something, they all know in Polacca before you've even woke up and told your friends.

'One time I fell off the mesa, not too far, only down about ten or twelve feet or so. It was at night and the police were chasing me. I'd been drinking I think. They never caught me though but I scratched up my face pretty bad. All my friends over there drink a lot – every day usually, there's nothing else to do. My friends make Kachina dolls too but I'm the only one that does pottery. My grandmother she taught me that. She does that all the time, she's really good, one of the best Hopi potters. She makes her own kiln. People come round all the time and give her orders.

'Some Anglos try to rip her off all the time. All sorts of rubbish they try to get her to take for her pottery. Cheap watches and stuff like that. Some Anglos even brought back a car once they said they would give her. We already threw them out once. You know I can't believe some of those people.'

Arnold put down his carving, dusted himself off and lay down on his bed. Sunlight streamed through the open hogan door and the rooster stood defiantly on the step quivering with pent-up aggression. I had the distinct feeling that the bird was not destined for old age.

'I was pretty drunk one time and came into my grandmother's house when these guys were trying to get some pots from her. I really let them have it and told them to get out. My grandmother got upset and said I shouldn't talk that way. I don't know about her – she's a pretty nice lady. You know she feeds anybody that comes round. That's the Hopi way I suppose but a lot of Anglos take advantage of that, they just come round at meal-times. My grandmother likes the old style food, chili and hominy stew. That's why I like to eat chili a lot I guess.

'I like working with people. At Polacca, up on the mesa we made our Kachina dolls together.' Arnold Youvella was cutting at the cottonwood root again. His long hair pulled back by a woven Hopi headband.

'We worked at a good steady pace there but over here it's hard to concentrate. This wood seems a bit soft, it's got knots as well, I should go down to San Carlos and get some better stuff. You know down there on the Apache reservation, they can be pretty rough those Apaches. The women are really bad – everyone says so. My father was living with this Apache woman – she hit him on the head with this big old frying-pan. He has this great big lump across the top of his forehead now. You know right up around the hairline. Boy, they're mean.

'When I was visiting my father down there he wouldn't let me go in the bar they have there. Only the Apaches and Zuni have a bar on their reservations. None of the other tribes down here do. Those Apaches fight a lot and kill each other sometimes.

'Damn, I've broke another leg off!' Arnold dipped the end of the broken leg in the white glue and stuck it back in place and then picked up another Kachina.

'Chet told me about you sneaking down to the Squaw Dance,' he laughed over his filing of a new leg.

'You could have gone down with him or Wayne. You were lucky some of those guys didn't jump you in the dark. They get pretty drunk some of them – and do stupid things. I go to a lot of dances out at Polacca. I think the Hopi have the most ceremonies. You wouldn't believe how many people get up on those mesas. Hopi, Navajos, tourists, everyone wandering around. The Hopi dancers they just get on with their ceremony. You get a lot of stupid people who think they can take photographs, even though they know the Hopi don't allow it.

'I took a camera off one guy. "Destroy the film" I told him but he gives me the camera, lens and everything. So I kept it. I think I pawned it in Gallup for thirty-five dollars, it was probably worth about four hundred. I never did get it out.'

'Polacca and some of those other mesas are getting really polluted now. They dump all the trash down the sides of the mesa. Crazy tourists stand up there on the top looking out saying how beautiful the view is. I say to them, "Look down at your feet". There's nothing but wine bottles and beer cans. Thousands of green wine bottles. That's all they drink up there. I don't know if they'll do anything about that. Probably not.

'My grandmother's house is really old. It's big. The walls are about three feet thick and made of stone. It's about twelve or thirteen feet to the ceiling and holding it up are really big logs twelve or thirteen inches thick. I sleep up on the roof all summer, it's good up there. I like that a lot.'

Outside stars hung in myriads and the valley was still. Warmer air was easing itself over Kin Li Chee and the Ganado ridge and soon the grass would begin to sprout and Irene's mother would bring the sheep back from their winter camp at Burnside.

High up, above the Anazazi cliff-dwellings the raven watched me come down the trail with my pack. Among the labyrinths of gullies and junipers I had lost the trail along the rims and had gone too far south. It had taken me an hour and a half of walking under a clear sky and a baking sun just to reach the head of the trail into the canyon.

Now tired, but happy at the prospect of returning to Canyon del Muerto, I began the twisting descent. As I came around a great wedge of rock the view opened and the wash and small bordering fields appeared below. Rich green rectangles of alfalfa covered the canyon floor. Snaking around the base of the scree cliff the irrigation ditch made a silver edge to the fields, until lost from sight around the thousand foot-high buttress at the neck of the side canyon of Twin Trails.

Spring had begun for the Navajo. As yet the cottonwoods were still grey-white with their swollen leaf buds waiting a little longer before opening. In thin lacy lines snow lay on the higher rock shelves and crevices of the canyon's east walls. Only in the late afternoon was the sun able to reach these places but as the sun rose higher each day the last signs of winter would quickly disappear.

Steadily I picked my way down, each turn of the trail showing more effects of spring. Small yellow and white flowers lay half-hidden among the piles of rocks and in the moister parts were clumps of a mauve wild sweet-pea. On my left, catching the full early afternoon sun, the Anazazi ruins basked in silence.

Halfway down the trail the clatter of dislodged rocks made me halt and, looking down, I made out the figure of a man leading a dun-coloured horse up through the shadows of an overhanging pine. The horse was pulling back against the halter rope, its hooves dislodging further fragments of rock, their rattle echoing back from the cliffs. As I moved lower and nearer the Navajo's two other loose horses shied away from cover. The horseman, perhaps in his middle twenties, wearing a dark high-crowned hat, then managed to mount the dun and began riding up the trail to where I now waited. Followed by the other two loose animals, a chestnut and a grey, he came up and we exchanged greetings. The Navajo explained that the horses had wintered in the canyon and although they were reluctant to leave, he was taking them out to his place on the rim.

'A lot of horses are left running around down there in the canyon during the winter,' Francis Draper had once commented. 'There's too many sometimes and in the ice and snow they can't find enough to eat. Pretty soon a few of those horses fall down. They don't get up no more.'

I carried on down the trail. When I reached the canyon floor I saw a familiar slightly hunched figure coming towards me across the sandy flat where the snow waters meet and seep down to the wash. It was William Wilson with his advance guard of five rangy dogs. Now alert, the dogs gave enthusiastic barks, recalling our last meeting in December down the canyon at Standing Cow.

William and I shook hands and he explained that he was busy irrigating Chester Hubbard's fields, the patches of fresh green I had seen from the trail head at the rim. Chester Hubbard, son-in-law to Henry and Garnet Draper, had fields adjoining theirs and these were next in the sequence of irrigation. In turn all the fields would be watered right on down the west side of the canyon as far as Standing Cow. The water was run from a dam further up the canyon near Big Cave. A ditch had been carefully cleared of débris during the winter, and in spring the water was channelled in turn to each person's land downstream. As each small set of fields received its water and became soaked, then the next Navajo farmer would open up his ditch system, water going where he directed until he was ready to release it to his neighbour's property and so on until the last people to bring life to their land would be Ella Draper's parents at Standing Cow.

Tommy and Francis Draper had irrigated their parents' land the week before and now William flooded the growing alfalfa in the next cluster of small fields.

'I go up to the spring to drink,' William pointed his ancient-looking brown hand behind me to a cement trough into which trickled spring water from the lower slopes of the trail canyon. Uninterested now, the dogs stood panting, silent, their thin bodies showing their rib cages.

'You see man with horse up there?' he looked up the trail.

'Yes,' I replied, 'three horses and one man.'

'Ah, three horses way up there, oh. O.K., I see you.'

Tails hanging limply, the thin dogs slowly followed William as he went to the spring and I covered the last quarter mile to the cabin.

Climbing over the barbed wire fence I went down the short slope and unlocked the cabin door. Inside it was much as I had left it in December except that now, on every piece of furniture and equipment, were far more mice droppings. Chopped wood lay before the old cook stove and a few blankets hung over the

Spring in the Canyon del Muerto

central cabin crossbeam, the only articles out of reach of the resident rodents.

Strips of roofing felt had been blown away in two places leaving chinks of sky visible from inside the cabin. The lamps had oil and the old iron bed was still there – it was good to be alone again in the cabin.

Taking the sooty kettle I went up to the spring and collected water before enjoying what I considered a well-earned rest. Lying on the old bed which offered only a mild twanging protest, I listened.

Through the open cabin door the dry rustle of a single cottonwood leaf dropped long ago in the fall broke the silence from the grove forty yards away. Inside the cabin a family of flies buzzed in the afternoon sun and one hit the wire window mesh with the force of a rifle across the canyon. From the wash came a multitude of voices, deep murmurs, the clink of ice, sounds like the bubbling laughter of children. Each sound remained separate, peculiar in its character. My hearing had become resensitized and the canyon's quiet was symphonic in its harmonics and chords.

Outside, there was an indigo sky perfect with its filling of stars, but inside the cabin things were far less tranquil. As soon as I lay down, an army of squeaking rodents moved out from every crack and hole. Invisible in the cabin's blackness they scrambled over every scalable surface, their progress traced by scratchings, rattling pans, gnawing and sudden bursts of conflict in the centre of the floor. Backed into the corner, my bed was under siege. At intervals the activity became so intense that I had to bang the metal bedhead and thump the wall. My impersonation of a snake hiss had no effect at all and it was soon apparent that I would have to share the cabin, the mice's tenancy far more permanent than mine.

A mouse ran over my head and I roared in protest to an unsympathetic uncaring audience – knowing its ineffectiveness. Finally, tired of listening to their antics, I cursed the mice and slept.

William Wilson was already irrigating the alfalfa fields when I walked along the slope above the cabin early the next morning. Water had been channelled into the next strip, the sections of land divided by low banks of earth. Each narrow field became a long tray into which the water poured.

The dogs lay inert, not showing the slightest interest in my passing. William took a large triangle of flat rock and dropped it upon its point into the main ditch of running water. Behind this, as the stream changed direction and started to flood another area, he back-filled with earth and removed the stone as the water accepted its new channel.

As I walked around the edge of the fields I passed the old collapsed hogan near the base of the cliff and continued south along the canyon, the busy sounds of the wash on my left. Horses, perhaps a dozen in all, wandered and grazed along the east bank, moving quietly through the pale brittle stalks of last year's bull-grass. Birds scattered through the wine-red dog-wood, calling, flocking in waves to seek out small cold insects. Dark brown and orange butterflies swooped gracefully down-stream, dipping down to the newly piled cottonwood branches flung across the rocks and sandbars. Up above me on the eastern rims a thousand feet from the wash the ledges and stunted junipers appeared a deep green-purple against a blue sky. Without a speck of cloud the canyon's roof was saturated with indescribable luminosity. Toward the west its intensity struck vibrations from the rock.

Set in the narrowing space between the canyon wall and the wash, the first hogan came into view with smoke curling up from its mud-domed roof. Just seen above a screen of six-foot-high dry grass, and perched at the edge of a slightly higher field the hogan sat in the morning sun, its door open. From some-where near the canyon wall came a scraping sound but whoever made it remained for the moment invisible.

A line of cottonwoods followed the wash to the first crossing place. On the bank above the water a group of small fields nestled beneath the west wall where a Navajo dug at the soil with his long-handled spade.

He was digging an irrigation ditch in preparation for his field's turn for the water. The man waved for me to come over, then leaned on his spade and explained his task.

'Now gonna irrigates this here field soon. Last year grew lots of beans over here.' He held up his hand, his thumb and fingers extended.

'Five sacks, those big one hundred pound gunny sacks. Lots a beans. Pretty good.'

I congratulated him on his efforts.

'You stayin' up there, eh? Henry Draper's place?'

'Yes,' I said. 'I'm a guest of the family. He lets me use the cabin now and again. This water is running high – makes it difficult to cross the wash.'

'Can't get over the wash, eh. Best you take your boots off, go across in your socks.' His eyes almost closed as he laughed loudly at his own humour and the good feelings of the morning. 'O.K. I see you now.' He put his foot to the spade and took the ditch a little further.

Another half a mile brought me to the limits of foot travel

along the canyon. Without great difficulty and most likely a good soaking, it was impossible to ford the wash. No sounds other than the rippling water disturbed the air of the canyon floor. As the freshly undercut banks dried in the sun the trickling sand was followed by clicking avalanches of pebbles, broken twigs and roots. Beneath an overhang flanked by several large boulders at the foot of the west cliff, and a short distance from where the wash had swung across and cut the trail, I found the ruins of an Anazazi dwelling.

The structure was small and probably little more than a storage area but scattered nearby on the sand were fragments of black and white decorated pottery. Beyond the remains among the willows and cottonwood trees a blue felt-roofed hogan sat in solitude, guarding the wide-mouthed box canyon. I had seen the hogan by chance the day before when mistakenly my line of travel had brought me to the rim above. Looking down to where I now stood I had seen a figure, only a dark speck from that height, moving across the canyon floor on the west side of the hogan. I now realised it had been William Wilson and this hogan was his summer camp.

Navajos with land and hogans in the canyons usually only visited their fields intermittently during the winter or not at all. Now the new cycle of planting, growing and harvesting had started, and they would spend more and more time in the canyon until summer held them there almost permanently.

At noon I came to the cabin again and after resting for a while followed the wash north along its west bank. This was higher ground, uneven and crossed by gullies draining the scree base of the canyon wall. Over the folds of the slopes I had a good view of the canyon floor in all directions.

A large number of horses grazed upon the green banks past the cottonwood grove, tolerant of me until I came within fifty yards of them. Curious but uncertain, the suspicious herd then pounded away along a high shelf above the wash on the opposite bank and disappeared among the willows.

'Sometimes you see wild goats right up along the ledges if you have binoculars,' Arnold informed me one night in the hogan. 'It's a long time, maybe three or four years since I was down there. I don't know why, but I haven't been over to my

Grandma's either.' He referred to Garnet Draper, his step-grandmother.

'Before they cleared all those trees up at the ranch I used to be over there a lot.'

I wondered about the goats and spent some time searching the distant ledges just below the rim. It was pointless of course. Even elephants would be difficult to see at that height with the camouflage of shadows among the junipers. Stones falling, rattling down from the scoured banks to the wash bed brought me out of my trance.

Often I wondered about my presence in the canyon. Sometimes I imagined myself from the heights of the canyon walls, watching my own antlike scale. Was I always watched? I knew that on previous occasions Navajos had watched me come and go but they had always revealed themselves one way or another. Not seeing anyone made me acutely aware of the advantages those heights had offered the Anazazi and Navajo when raiders had entered their homelands. Whenever I found myself staring into the shallow wash, I half-expected to see the reflection of a Navajo moving darkly alongside my own. Anazazi ghosts must surely live here.

A horseman passed the cottonwoods going towards the rim trail before the night shadows were set. Muffled by the soft earth, the hoof beats faded and were gone.

The smell of piñon resin spilled from the black stove chimney pipe and drifted over the wash. I sat on the cabin step while the whisperings of the water comforted the horses as they made ready for the night. Scurrying on the skunk listened too, and even the buzzard took time to pause and rested from its silent flight along the canyon.

Night had a peculiar unworldliness in the canyon. Its magic seemed unsoiled by any suggestion of reality.

'Yaatey,' I called out to Archie Francis. He was perched on a rock at the edge of the sand flats by the spring and he wore an incongruous construction worker's yellow hard hat. Two days before he had stood in Garnet Draper's kitchen wearing his enormous black stetson. Now he watched out for his flock.

Archie returned my greeting and I told him I was staying in the cabin.

'Is Tommy over there?' he said, looking out over the sand flat

to the rocks where the sheep and goats had secreted themselves.
'The last I heard he had gone to Chinle,' I replied. Archie
was smiling wryly and gazing at the rocks. He knew as I did
that Tommy had called on the bootlegger.

'Oh, he finished irrigation maybe!' Archie's face gave the
barest clue to the depth of his amusement.

Sliding from the boulder, Archie gave a grunt of conclusion
and limped off awkwardly towards the sheep.

Turning, I followed the canyon trail running past the derelict
hogan where another mixed flock grazed in an untilled field
next to Chester Hubbard's irrigated land. Standing among the
animals was a short stocky red-capped Navajo. I called out in
passing and the man replied in English, asking where I was
going. 'Just walking down the canyon,' I said and then as I was
unable to understand his further questioning I climbed through
the fence and approached him.

As I came nearer to the man he began to sing in Navajo. He
faced me, moving from side to side and singing the rising and
falling song of the Squaw Dance, the Enemy Way.

Its effect was to remove all sights and sounds from my
attention except the Navajo. Hypnotically almost, I walked up
to the Indian and as I covered the last few yards he stopped
singing, greeted me and shook my hand.

'Ho, I am William Draper. Some call me William, some
Willat.' His broad face widened further as he laughed and
scuffed the earth with his foot.

'Henry Draper, he's my uncle.' He continued laughing. 'Just
one of those many family lines.'

'Watch out for the dog,' he said looking over his shoulder.
'He's around here somewhere. Probably hiding behind a rock
or bush – you go down the canyon, eh? Past William Wilson's
place, yes.'

William, sometimes Willat, spoke English well, without the
heavy accent or poor construction of many of the older Navajos.

'That old boy Wilson, he's an early bird that one. I met him
coming out of the canyon way up on the trail near the rim about
six thirty this morning. He'd already been down to check the
irrigating. He's a wiry old devil. He goes on steady like that all
day.'

The sheep had started to scatter towards the wash and

headed gradually upstream. It was time for William to follow.
'Ho, I see you sometime. We'll probably just follow the sheep
up the canyon and make camp up there somewhere. We go just
like that, when the sheep kind of move over there.'

As predicted the flock quite suddenly started again and the
jovial figure of the singing Navajo followed as I continued on
around the corner of the great cliff.

The hogan I had observed the day before perched on the
knoll above the yellow bull grass stood with its door open, but
now a man sat on its step. He saw me coming along the trail and
stood up when I waved to him.

Spread along the edge of the fence were masses of small
mauve flowers, a startling colour against the sun-bleached
reeds and sand. A few sheep crackled among the dry grasses
and as I drew level with the hogan the Navajo walked down
towards me. We shook hands at the fence and when I talked he
made the sign that he spoke only Navajo. Even so, I explained
my reasons for being there, perceiving that he seemed to
understand some of my words. Unfortunately, I failed to
understand his and having shaken hands a second time he
smiled and moved back towards the canyon wall with his dogs
and sheep.

I watched him go, listening to the brittle bull-grass and
feeling the sun across my shoulders. Soon I would leave Canyon
del Muerto and the high country of the Navajos. For some
indefinable reason I had never felt a complete stranger among
these mountains and canyons. Distant red-edged mesas always
lined the horizon with grandeur but they never appeared to be
completely new to me – as though I had seen them before.
Many times the land and the manners of its people made an
impression that was more to do with an ancient memory than
the revelation of new experience. All through the wanderings of
The People from the mountains of the north their strength was
held by their love of the earth and its forces. In the canyons and
across the mesas the stories of Crow Man's people had soaked
the land and become part of the earth itself.

The shadow of the raven passed along the corrugations of the
trail. In silence the shadow flew up into the cottonwood and
called out, splintering the sunlight.

Snows and blue shadows stayed too long on the eastern

ramparts of the canyon for the Anazazi to use its ledges for their homes. They, like the Navajo, had but one major concern for that side of the canyon and that was to see the sun rise daily above its rim. As in all early religions and those of modern times which ally themselves to nature, the Indians of the Americas saw in the great shining disc the power of their universe. In its existence lay the perpetuity of the people and of the tribe. Its strength was their strength and it followed The People's way. They in return worshipped its eternal simplicity and beauty.

All things of the air and the earth were sacred mysteries and only by revering the spirits of those things would the people live. Spirits of creatures who were not men and those who made the wind and rain, those who decided how and when a leaf should fall, it was they who held the key to life: the circle. Through them the Great Father spirit knew The People.

Looking back towards the cottonwoods for the last time I said goodbye in spirit to my friend from last winter, the black-coated scarecrow. It leaned heavily from the buffeting of the canyon winds but it now faced the west rim. I discovered that Bill Draper had been the figure's maker and as I walked out to the trail its red trailing scarf whipped out in a goodnatured gesture. At least I accepted it as such and went on.

Archie Francis was still up near the Anazazi ruins at Twin Trails when I began the climb. It was late afternoon and the sun shone on my left side. Archie watched me start the trail before following the sheep and goats to the shadowed mouth of the box canyon. He limped behind the flock and looking down at him I wondered what he had thought about all day.

Old William Wilson had gone somewhere, leaving the irrigation water still rushing on to the alfalfa. He had either gone back to the rim again or was perhaps attending to his own land downstream. Wherever he was, he would be flanked by his pack of dogs and would spend his days walking from rim to canyon floor and back until he died. To a Navajo of the old times, to breathe was to work and the hardship was so constant that its meaning was forgotten.

As I neared the rim two young boys with moon faces and long

streaming black hair raced down the trail with the agility of goats. I waited while they passed, their run never faltering as they disappeared among the rocks below. From the head of the trail I saw them finally emerge from the shadows at the bottom and, still at a lope, they crossed the sand flat to where Archie Francis watched his sheep.

Once up on the rim I headed north-west over great mounds of folded rock and through gullies with pools of clear water. This time my bearings were correct and I reached the small canyon that I had explored a few days earlier. Struggling on I eventually came to the old sweat house and then over the last shelves of rock to Henry Draper's land.

The little ranch house, as always, showed no sign of life but when I knocked and entered I was welcomed by old Henry. He and Garnet sat in the silent bedroom.

'Yaatey. How you like it down the canyon this time?' Garnet shifted her seat a fraction.

I told them first of the mice in the cabin. The couple laughed, then Henry lay across the double bed at right angles to its length with his hands supporting the back of his head.

'Yes,' Garnet said. 'We were only saying yesterday that you would have a lot of company down there at night. I don't know why there's so many of those creatures now. Last year we got rid of them all.'

Henry chipped in, peering over his thick spectacles, 'We trap them all the time in the summer. I think they must have stored a lot of corn in there.'

They wanted to know if I had seen anyone down in the canyon and I described those I had met.

'Ah,' frowned Garnet, 'that Archie Francis was down there with the sheep, eh?'

I asked them about his limp.

'Oh, he got his feet frozen. They cut one off and half the other. He got drunk and passed out in the snow a couple of years ago. That's what happened to him. It didn't stop him drinking though. He's always getting drunk that man.'

We talked a while, then I left for Chinle. That night I stayed with Francis and Ella.

'Nothing really happens since we last saw you. Usually there's something like the branding or big storm or stuff like that.' Francis always spoke as though he were trying to make himself heard above the noise of something else, even when he was close to the listener.

'So you really have a good time in the canyon? I went down with my horse last week, doing some irrigating down there. In the spring we do that. My Mom and Dad's cabin, it needs fixin' up. All that roofin' stuff got blown off in those winds.

'It's those cottonwoods, they make the wind come down like that. Pretty soon I'll chop some of those down.'

Francis, like his mother and father, was curious about who I had seen in the canyon. I told him of those I knew and those I had seen for the first time.

'Archie Francis, yes, he's the one they had to cut the foot off. That crazy guy, he was out around here in Chinle. I think he went to sleep in a ditch after he had too much to drink. He's drinking all the time. That other fella, William Draper, his name used to be Brown Moustache Begay but a couple of years ago he changed it to Draper. I don't know why he did that. Years ago he used to be a really good medicine man in the Del Muerto area. Then he really got involved with the Catholic church and he had a good job over at Round Rock. He was janitor for the church and everything. Then he took off with some other woman, left his wife over there. After that he said the church was no good and never had anything else to do with it.

'Sometime after that he separated from that other woman and went back to Del Muerto. Now I think he becomes a medicine man again. I was over that way and happened to stop at Squaw Dance over there and he was really singing. He knows all the songs. I think that's what he is now when people need him, a medicine man.

'He drinks too and doesn't have a job no more. Those sheep he had down in the canyon, they weren't his. Some of the people at Del Muerto pay him some money to look after them. He lives with his sister now.

'You see that's what is happening to lots of Navajos. They don't know which way to go. Over there they see something good and then maybe over here they see something else. They're not sure about things no more.'

Night outside was sharp and dry with a sky empty of cloud

An earth and log-roofed hogan in the Canyon del Muerto

but full of winking stars. Competition among the local dogs moved from peaks of full-throated choruses to staccato high-pitched yapping. The reservation teemed with dogs, each family owning at least two or three animals and as family groupings enlarged so the packs became more numerous.

'Even in religions we got lots of mixed-up things. Like I said before about the jewellery, all the turquoise and silver is buried with the dead, 'specially the things belonging to the medicine men. When they die all their stuff goes with them.

'People spend a lot of money on burying their relatives, even when they can't afford it. Sometimes they have to borrow too much. They buy a real expensive suit and shoes with other sorts of things which the dead person liked. Rugs, baskets, jewellery, even guns and horses if it's a man.

'When my friend who used to go everywhere with me on the rodeos got killed in an auto crash his parents bought everything new for his burial. A new saddle, spurs, ropes, chaps and belts, real expensive boots too. All those things were new but that's the way the people feel.

'As well as those things and a special casket they brought his best horse over to the grave and shot it right there, then they buried it with him.

'It is quite a normal thing for a person to be buried with his horse. Two or three weeks ago they did that up at Del Muerto in the cemetery there. People who belong to the various churches still do these things. When the Presbyterian minister or the Catholic priest has finished the service the relatives bring over the horse and shoot. Then maybe they fill in the grave with a tractor or something. It's the way.

'A guy just over here,' Francis went on, 'he knew he was going to die and told his people that he wanted to be buried just in his ordinary clothes because he was a poor man. It didn't make no difference though. His family just went ahead when he died and put all new things on him and all kinds of stuff with his body.

'People are still very superstitious about dying. They don't want the person's ghost coming back and causing bad things against them. So, they want that dead person to have everything so he can't say they didn't care about him.

'Sometimes when a person dies in the hogan the family move out and build a new hogan and let the old one fall down. Like this old lady who died just down from my Dad's place. They buried her in the floor of the hogan and then pushed the roof in on top of the grave.

'When somone dies no one in the family will touch the body or have anything to do with it. They pay the medicine man and maybe one or two other persons outside the family to take the body out and all those other things.

'Up there on the rims around the canyons you can still see those places where they used to bury The People. They put the dead person down in a big crack in the rocks and then piled rocks over the top so that the coyote and other animals can't dig up the bones. Well, that's how we used to do it, now we use the cemetery – mostly.'

Saying goodbye to the family was sad and difficult. I made these last journeys to the family members scattered over a radius of forty miles, with both the burden of ending and the satisfaction of having made so many friends.

Harry Shandi, the leader of the team of Yeibechai dancers who had come out of the winter night at Sunrise Mesa spoke to me last of all.

'The medicine men say that the first thunder has been heard and the first lightning seen, the winter ceremonies can no longer be held. Night Chants, the Yeibechai Ceremony and the Fire Dance can only be performed while the snakes sleep and the spider hibernates. From April until November the Enemy Way, the Squaw Dance, brings The People together for the ways of our religion.

'I cannot speak of the Yeibechai now. It is forbidden in our religion to discuss these things now that the performing of the Yeibechai has come to an end.

'The songs must be learned from the medicine men, they cannot be told. We can only know them from the early times in that way.'

There was a cold wind and the dust flew across the open places in the morning. At the red base of the mesa, stretched out thin and bare, dust devils played on the warming earth. Some withered and died seconds after their birth while occasionally a monster corkscrewed into giant proportions as it moved slowly north. One whirling column of wind and dust came out of the dry wastes and grew quickly into a sucking spout. A distant hogan and its corrals fell beneath its shuddering storm of flying grit and twigs. Strips of tin and paper, sacks, empty boxes and other débris rose up and spun away in the churning air. The brown inverted cone attempted to drill itself into the flat scrubland where its strength was sapped into gradual defeat.

A hundred feet high the devil thinned slowly into a pale yellow cloud, débris falling back to earth, the blue sky now still and clean.

An indefinable feeling of a long-past relationship with this high country and its people remained with me. Sagebrush crackled faintly against the push of the wind while my thoughts were drawn out through the familiar bones of the landscape. Along the horizon the sacred mountains marked the limit of Navajo country. These now seemed my own boundaries between my life among The People and the life to which I must return.

'We listen to the piñon and watch the ways of the spiders,' say the old men. 'From the ancient creatures came our life and our love of the land.'

Along the damp arroyo horses thudded through pools of slick light and dark. For a moment longer my shadow etched the red soil and then from the mesa I watched a solitary crow fly away towards the dark mountain in the west.

Index

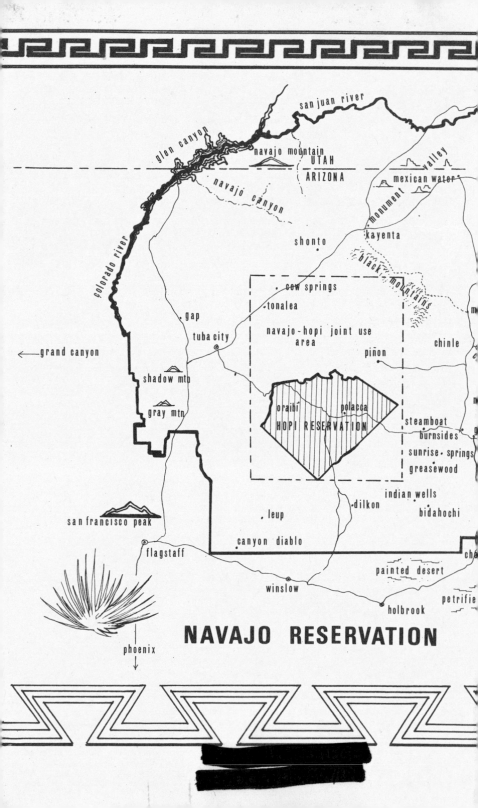

NAVAJO RESERVATION